Selby Albert Moran

100 Valuable Suggestions to Shorthand Students

Third Edition

Selby Albert Moran

100 Valuable Suggestions to Shorthand Students
Third Edition

ISBN/EAN: 9783744744249

Printed in Europe, USA, Canada, Australia, Japan

Cover: Foto ©Thomas Meinert / pixelio.de

More available books at **www.hansebooks.com**

ONE HUNDRED

VALUABLE SUGGESTIONS

TO

SHORTHAND STUDENTS.

A COMPILATION OF IMPORTANT FACTS RELATING TO
EVERY BRANCH OF THE STUDY AND PRAC-
TICE OF SHORTHAND WRITING.

SPECIALLY ARRANGED FOR STUDENTS, TEACHERS, AND
YOUNG REPORTERS OF ALL SYSTEMS.

BY

SELBY A. MORAN,

UNIVERSITY OF MICHIGAN,
PRINCIPAL OF THE STENOGRAPHIC INSTITUTE,
ANN ARBOR.

THIRD EDITION.

ANN ARBOR, MICHIGAN:
PUBLISHED BY THE AUTHOR.
1890.

PREFACE.

It may seem presumptuous on the part of the author to place before the public a work of this kind when there are so many others whose more varied experience far better fits them for such an undertaking.

Feeling, however, that others who have written works relating to Shorthand have almost wholly neglected to render to the student and young reporter the special help which this little volume is intended to give, and believing that there is a real demand for a work of this kind, the author makes no further apology for its appearance.

The aim of this work is to render assistance to students of all systems of Shorthand by a series of suggestions concerning important facts only a few of which have ever found a place in any text-book, yet facts which every student should keep constantly in mind. As such, it is believed that it will prove especially serviceable to that large class of students who are undergoing a course of self-instruction. Since that which has been written heretofore, in the same line of the present work, has been confined almost wholly to court and newspaper reporting, more attention is given to amanuensis reporting, a new branch of the profession which has, of late years, far outstripped all the others, both in its numbers and requirements.

Simplicity of expression has been kept constantly in view, that the book may be used by the student for general dictation work as soon as all the principles are learned. It is hoped that, in this way, it will serve a double purpose; not only to give the student many valuable hints in regard to his study and practice, but also to furnish suitable material for speed work, whereby facts which every Short-hand student should know may be fixed more firmly in mind.

That the contents of this little volume may assist that large number of young men and women who are deter-mined to win success in the practice of this beautiful art, is earnestly hoped.

To the many kind friends who have so freely placed at his disposal the valuable lessons learned in their long ex-perience as reporters, and especially to that one who, by constant encouragement, has proven an inspiring genius, not only in this, but also in other and more difficult under-takings, this work is respectfully inscribed by

THE AUTHOR.

STENOGRAPHIC INSTITUTE
Ann Arbor, Mich., May, 1886.

NOTE TO THE SECOND EDITION.

When the first edition of this little book was placed before the public, it was with some feeling of uncertainty as to whether there was need of such a work. That there should be a demand for a second edition almost within a twelvemonth after the first was published, is certainly more than the author expected. It plainly shows that there is a demand for a work of this kind, and to supply this demand a new edition is offered to the public.

S. A. M.

STENOGRAPHIC INSTITUTE, September, 1887.

INTRODUCTION.

Shorthand is a beautiful theory and a successful art as well. To acquire a knowledge of the theory is one thing, to put this theory into practice is another.

The text-books on the various systems of Shorthand writing have given a general explanation of the principles of these systems, but have omitted many important facts relative to learning the art, and are almost entirely silent upon the practical application of Shorthand. In presenting these facts which are intended to cover this neglected part of the student's work, it has been thought best to arrange them in the following order:

   I. Suggestions for students before beginning the study.
I—XVII.

  II. Suggestions for students while pursuing the study.
XVIII—XLV.

 III. Suggestions concerning the necessity of learning to read Shorthand.
XLVI—L.

 IV. Suggestions relative to increasing speed.
LI—LIX.

  V. Suggestions for the Amanuensis.
LX—LXXII.

 VI. Suggestions for Court, Newspaper, Convention, and Speech Reporters.
LXXIII—LXXXIII.

VII. General Suggestions for all Reporters.
LXXXIV—C.

The student who will give a little careful attention to the suggestions coming under the first heading may be assured that his chances of success in learning the art will be much greater than if he were left to depend entirely upon his own resources.

During the course of his study he will receive much real help from the suggestions under the second, third, and fourth headings. By applying them in practice to those points to which they refer, the study will prove much more interesting and far better results will be obtained.

Under the heading for Amanuensis Reporters, the student will receive some very material assistance. These suggestions carefully followed out, will save many disagreeable experiences to the young reporter and enable him to do much more satisfactory work.

So much has been written upon the different branches of reporting given under the sixth heading that but two or three suggestions are devoted to each of them. In these are given those points which will prove of the greatest help to the reporter who aspires to success in any of these lines of work.

In the last division, under the heading of General Suggestions, have been grouped those hints which reporters in any branch of the profession will find it advantageous to know.

SHORTHAND STUDENTS.

I. Have Faith in Shorthand.*

There is probably no other one thing that has caused so many people to fail in their endeavors to become reporters as a lack of confidence in Shorthand. Too often we hear beginners say: "I will try it and see whether I can succeed or not." The young man or woman, who, after seeing that thousands of others have made a success of Shorthand, cannot say, "I *will* succeed," had better not spend time or money upon it, or, in fact, upon anything else that requires a little study and application.

To become a fair reporter is no Herculean task demanding the work of years, and then to be acquired by only a "born few."

Shorthand has been greatly improved of late years, and is based upon real scientific principles. Any one with only ordinary ability can master it and become able to write from four to six times faster than in longhand.

Do not doubt the merits of Shorthand, but rather say, "I will succeed." You can, if you will, make it an acquirement

---

* See note immediately following the last Suggestion.

that will be of much value to you every day of your life. If you will only throw your whole soul into the work and believe that you can do what many others, no smarter than yourself, have done, you need have no fears of making a failure.

II. Take a Course of Instruction in some School.

You may, by your own individual efforts, be able to succeed in becoming an expert reporter, but the chances certainly are against you. There is, to my mind, no doubt whatever as to the truth of the statement that not one in one hundred succeed in their efforts to master the art unaided. On the other hand, my experience has been that not one in twenty-five makes a failure when they conscientiously pursue the course under a competent teacher. This may seem to conflict with statements made in another suggestion wherein it is stated that the student, by finding it necessary to have a teacher, will come to depend upon his help. This, however, is not the case since the true work of a teacher is to guide the efforts of the pupil in the right direction and in this way make him more self-reliant. Although the aim of this little volume is to supply in a permanent form the valuable suggestions that a teacher would make to a student and to assist, as far as possible, those who are unable to have the help of a teacher, yet no book can be made to cover every individual case, much less to arouse an enthusiasm in the work that an earnest teacher and fellow students will inspire. There are, however, many young people who are anxious to learn Shorthand but who are so situated that attending a school is entirely out of the question. Such will find that the next best course to pursue is to take lessons by mail from some of the schools that are doing excellent work in that line. There are none to whom the mails are not accessible and who may not in this way receive much valuable assistance.

III. Shorthand Schools Guaranteeing Positions to Students are Frauds.

It is true that many schools are able to render considerable assistance to their pupils in helping them to secure positions, but to guarantee places at a certain time is perfectly absurd. Parties who have no interest in the school whatever are the ones who have the say in giving the students situations.

If the young man who contemplates taking a course in some Shorthand school will give the matter a moment's thought, he will see the fallacy of such offers. It is expected, by such inducements, to deceive a class of young people who do but little thinking for themselves. We would be much more willing to recommend a school which positively stated in its advertisements that it did not guarantee situations to its graduates than one which offered everything and charged accordingly. This class of schools is, as a rule, of mushroom growth. It is impossible for them to fulfill their promises since they have no positions actually at their disposal and, also, because the class of students drawn to such schools are not usually of the kind likely to become able to fill good positions. It does not take long to detect such frauds, after which they soon disappear. It is much safer to attend a school that has maintained its reputation through a long series of years.

IV. Do not be Discouraged by the Cry of an Over-Supply.

The young man or woman who takes up the study of Shorthand will surely be compelled to endure the constant cry that there is an over-supply. To be sure there is an "over-supply" of Shorthand writers. So is there an over-supply of workmen in every industrial pursuit, yet people go on learning the various trades just as though the cry had never been heard. The over-supply comes from that large class who do things only by halves. We have all heard the cry of an over-supply of lawyers, teachers, carpenters, blacksmiths, etc.; yet a good lawyer, teacher, or carpenter is never out of employment and at a loss for something to do. You never hear of a man who stands well up in his business or profession making any complaint about the competition which he may have. People who can do their part well are always in demand. Of course there will always be poor reporters, just as there are poor workmen in all vocations in life. These will always stand in the way of those who can do good work, but prove yourself to be deserving, and you will have no trouble in pushing past them. The demand for *competent* Shorthand reporters and type-writer operators is rapidly on the increase. No one can better judge of this increasing demand than those who have been, for a long time, engaged in supplying the calls for this kind of work, and these will invariably tell you that the demand has increased many hundred per cent. in the past few years, and is likely to increase at the same rate in the years to come. It is true that the number studying Shorthand is proportionally large. The only effect of this, however, will be a demand for a higher standard of proficiency in those practicing the art. Ambitious students need have no fear because of this, since the standard is not likely to be so high that any one, with a fair amount of common sense, may not reach it.

The day may come, although we doubt it, when there will be an over-supply of good reporters, but if ever, it is so far in the future that no one now living need have the least fear of being thus crowded.

V. More Depends upon Yourself Than upon Any One Else.

There is no surer way to success in any undertaking than by a firm reliance upon self. This applies with especial force to the study of Shorthand. The most successful reporters we have ever known were those who did not depend upon the help of teacher or friend to learn Shorthand for them, but relied upon their own ability to succeed. *Real determination* will go as far, if not farther, than natural endowments, hence he who will rely upon the former may have as much or even more hope of success than one who is otherwise naturally fitted for the work but lacks self-reliance. There are now too many "hangers on" in the reporting business. This is very sure to result in failure when one is obliged to cut loose from all former support and act for himself. Resolve that you will do what others, no more capable than yourself have done, and then *go ahead and do it.*

VI. Do Not be Influenced by the Advice of People Who Know Nothing about Shorthand.

Nothing is more absurd than to hear a certain class of people decrying Shorthand when, in fact, they know nothing at all about it. We have known many young people who would have become excellent reporters had they not been induced to give up the idea of learning Shorthand by the advice of persons who had never before even heard of Stenography.

In a court of justice the testimony of a witness would be rejected at once were it concerning matters of which he had no knowledge whatever. This same principle ought to hold good in everything. If you wish advice in regard to the reporting business, ask it of some one who is competent to advise you intelligently. It will be found that those who have given the subject enough attention to enable them to speak authoritatively are the ones, with rare exceptions, who have made a success of it and who will advise you to begin the study and stick to it. Also, do not allow yourself to be influenced against Shorthand by those who pretend to know all about it, but who, in fact, cannot answer a sensible question concerning the art.

VII. Ladies Should not Hesitate about Learning Shorthand.

Shorthand writing is a very artistic work and, as such, is well suited to the finer nature and more delicate organization of womankind. Judging from the large number of ladies who have entered the Stenographic field and from the excellent satisfaction which is almost always given, I see no reason why any lady should hesitate for a moment to accept this calling, if she feels the necessity of engaging in any kind of employment. The work is light, interesting, and in every sense respectable. Of course there are kinds of Stenographic work which would be distasteful to ladies, but these are only a very small portion of the places where Shorthand is used. Large commercial houses, railroad offices, insurance offices, banks, and other places where a large correspondence is conducted, the offices of professional men, editorial rooms, and all places where original documents are prepared, offer excellent opportunities for ladies, and in many places they are preferred to gentlemen. As compared with teaching it is far more desirable.

VIII. The Student can do Much Better by Having a Fellow-Student with Whom to Practice.

Shorthand, unlike most other studies, is not one in which the student can succeed quite as well, or better by studying alone than he can by working with some fellow-student. Learning Shorthand consists, for the most part, in constant practice; and the nearer this practice approaches actual reporting, the better it is. A person may learn to do rapid work in Shorthand and practice only by copying, but this is quite different from following a speaker. By copying, he gets his matter in sentences or parts of sentences, and learns to give his whole attention to writing, but when he comes to follow a speaker he finds it entirely different. He does not receive a sentence at a time, the speaker pausing until that has been written. The words come in a steady flow, one sentence immediately following another, whether the reporter is ready or not. He must learn not only to give off that which has been received, but also to receive constantly new words and retain them in his memory until they are written. The good reporter as a rule, closely follows the speaker, but he should also be able to retain fifteen or twenty words, or even more at once, so that in case of an unexpected spurt on the part of the speaker he will not lose a single word. Since the practical work of the reporter consists entirely in following a speaker, the more practice of this kind he gets the better qualified he will be. By taking the course with some other student and the two dictating the exercises to each other, actual reporting will come much easier. There is no doubt but that many who learn Shorthand by themselves and fail when they come to try actual reporting, could trace the cause to having learned to copy and not to report.

IX. In the Beginning of Your Practice Use Paper Properly Ruled.

This is quite essential, for two reasons. First. Students are apt to get into the habit of making the characters of uneven length. They do not see the disadvantage of this until they come to the double length and the half length letters, a device made use of in most systems of Shorthand writing. Unless the student has become accustomed to writing the characters of nearly uniform length, he will be sure to have difficulty sooner or later. And what is more, a habit once formed is much harder to overcome than it is to learn the right way in the first place. The most successful method we have tried in order to secure uniformity in the length of letters is to use paper ruled both ways, so that the squares formed will be the right size for a letter of medium or standard length. The beginner should strictly adhere in his practice to the use of this kind of paper, allowing each character to correspond with the size of the square. One or two weeks of this kind of drill, at first, will develop uniformity in the handwriting sufficiently to enable one to use ordinary reporting paper with no danger of difficulty resulting.

Second. Students are apt, in the beginning, to write their letters a third longer than necessary. This not only makes their work look cumbersome and is a waste of paper, but takes more time. The principal object of Shorthand is to save time, and the writer who makes his characters longer than necessary defeats, in a large measure, the efforts he is putting forth to save time. A small, plain handwriting should be cultivated from the very beginning, as it not only looks neater but is a saving of much valuable time. The student, and the reporter as well, should use paper ruled with purple lines, as they are distinct at night as well as in daylight, and also show plainly horizontal characters written upon them. Paper ruled with pale red lines should not be used, as the lines are apt to be so dim that to follow them would be too great a strain upon the eyesight while writing at night.

Shorthand students will also find it advantageous to use paper uniform as to width of ruling. This will help very considerably in enabling one to maintain uniformity in the length of letters, since most writers gauge the size of their characters to a large extent by the width of the spaces between the lines. If the spaces differ in width, one will form the habit of varying upright letters while the horizontal letters will remain unchanged.

X. Be Careful as to the Position of the Light by Which You are Writing.

As a rule, the first thing to fail the scribe is his eyesight. This is generally caused by neglecting to pay attention to the position of the light by which he writes. This is especially the case while writing at night and using gas or an oil lamp. The position from which the least injury will result is the one which admits the light upon the paper without either shining directly into the eyes, or casting a reflection into them from the paper upon which one is writing. Such position of the light as brings about either of these results should be scrupulously avoided as both are very injurious to the eyes. The best results of lighting the paper may be obtained by using a shaded light placed in front and far enough to the left so as not to throw the reflection into the eyes.

With the lamp in this position and shaded low enough to protect the eyes, little trouble will follow. The light should also be strong enough to light the paper and ruling very distinctly, but not so strong as to dazzle the eyes. As a rule, more trouble comes from having too much light than from having too little. Another very important feature is, that the light should be a steady one and always kept at a uniform distance from the place of writing. By becoming accustomed to a light just strong enough to make it appear as much like daylight as possible, and in proper position so as not to injure the eyes by direct or indirect light, one will find but little inconvenience from the very great amount of night work which every reporter is obliged to do from time to time.

The position of the light when using the Type-writer is also important. It should be placed so as to throw the light fully on the front of the machine, and be high enough to light the keyboard plainly. This can be done to the best advantage by having the light either to the left or right, according to the position of your copy, and about as high as the shoulder. It should be shaded so as not to throw any light whatever upon the operator.

XI. Learn to Pronounce Distinctly.

The student can hardly expect to become a correct writer in representing words by sound signs unless he can first pronounce the words correctly, or, what is more difficult, correct the mistakes made by the speaker whom he is following.

The English language, so far as pronunciation is concerned and, in fact, in every other respect, is by no means a scientific one. Being composed of so many elements, there can be no rules of pronunciation which will apply even to a very small class of words. Still, with a little care and a reference to the dictionary when any uncertainty exists, little or no difficulty will be experienced with the majority of the more commonly occurring words.

XII. Use a Pen Suited to Your Particular Touch.

The idea of having all conform to a particular style and especially to a particular number of pen is perfectly absurd. It would be quite as reasonable to require all reporters to wear the same sized hat or shoes. We sometimes see advertisements of some special kind of pen, not even including different numbers of the same make, which is recommended as just the thing for *all* students of Shorthand. Yet people buy them, and the lady whose touch is the most delicate vainly endeavors to do good work with the same kind of pen made use of by the sturdy young man who has just forsaken his maul at the rail pile and

2

begun to draw curves and make hooks. The pen to use is the one best suited to your particular touch. Any person of ordinary ability will have no difficulty in deciding what particular pen suits his hand and with which he can do the best work. There are, however, some styles of pens totally unfit for any one to use in reporting, while there are some brands among the different numbers of which, almost anybody may find one suited to his hand. A good gold pen is by far the best to use in Shorthand work. It is always ready for use and, if properly taken care of, will last for years of steady writing.

XIII.   It is Quite Necessary that the Reporter be Able to Write a Plain Longhand.

It is commonly believed that the practice of Shorthand will so affect one's longhand as to make it almost illegible. This belief is caused by the fact that Shorthand writers are generally very poor scribes. Their poor writing, however, is not caused, to any extent, by the mere writing of Shorthand. The poor longhand writing, so common among reporters is, in almost every case, the result of rapid writing in making transcripts. The same result would be brought about by mere copying even though the writer had never made a Shorthand character.

Now that the type-writer is used almost exclusively in transcribing Shorthand notes there is no excuse at all for a reporter not being a good longhand writer. It very frequently occurs that the amanuensis, especially, will have more or less writing to do with the pen. Some part of his type-writer may give out and he will be obliged to use the pen until it is repaired. It also frequently occurs that some particular letter or paper is required to bo written in longhand, or, it may be, copied in some book where the type-writer cannot be used. Oftentimes blanks aro to be filled out whero it is necessary to use the pen. Newspaper and court reporters may not always bo ablo to have a type-writer at hand, and will then be obliged to resort to longhand writing. There are numerous other contingencies that may arise in which the reporter will bo expected to use the old method. In order to givo satisfaction, ho should be able to write readily a plain longhand, for, since type-writing has become so common, peoplo aro not apt to have much patience with longhand unless it is executed nearly, if not quite, as plainly as typo-written matter.

XIV. Learn to Punctuate.

Although there are very few, if any, punctuation marks used in any system of Shorthand, yet it is quito essential that the reporter should know when to use the more common ones, since he has occasion to use them every timo he makes a transcript of his notes. It is truo that thero is, in the main, but littlo uniformity in punctuation; yet there are some general principles which aro accepted by all. These should bo understood by all Shorthand writers. This would avoid much of the wretched work which is often seen in type-written matter and which, in that form, stands out in such a marked way.

It would be well for every Shorthand student, not pre-viously prepared in this respect, to secure some treatise on punctuation and make a thorough study of it. There are various works on the subject, any of which contains many valuable suggestions and is well worth a careful study.

They may be had for a few cents each and no Shorthand writer should be without one.

XV. Learn to Spell.

This, to some, may seem to be a very useless suggestion; but any one who has an opportunity and will look over a few type-written letters, such as are sent out by many large business firms where Stenographic secretaries are employed, would think otherwise. One would be inclined to think that each reporter spelled his words according to the dictates of his own fancy and that his fancy was constantly varying. The use of the type-writer shows errors in spelling very plainly, and the endeavor which is made by many to cover up the mistakes only makes a bad matter worse.

Business men are, as a rule, aware of this failing on the part of reporters, and are apt to treat with disfavor all applicants who cannot prove their ability to spell correctly the more common English words. The advice generally given to poor spellers is, "Always look up a word in the dictionary unless you are sure that you are right." This advice will apply in some cases, but too often it occurs that one is sure he is right when he is about as far wrong as he could very well be. The great trouble is that, since the old fashioned spelling school has become a thing of the past, very little effort is made by young people to acquire proficiency in this important branch of education. One of the necessary things in becoming a good type-writer operator is an ability to spell without a particle of hesitation every word that may be used. That is, in itself, quite an accomplishment. If one cannot spell readily, much valuable time will be lost in hesitating or in looking up words in the dictionary. We would advise every young reporter to give special attention to this point as it is well worth the while.

XVI. Use the Best Quality of Ink.

There is about as much difference between the various kinds of ink that are generally kept for sale as there is between a charcoal pencil and a good gold pen. And what is worse, very few people have any idea that there can be any difference in ink. Any liquid that will make a colored mark, even though it be only indigo water, is, to the majority of people, just as good as the best writing fluid. Good ink is just as essential as good pens and paper. Ink that flows evenly and freely from the pen should be used. It should also be such as will make distinct lines when the writing is being done and not become either lighter or darker after use.

There are many kinds of ink which do this, and the Shorthand writer whose system includes both light and shaded lines (and this is the case with the majority of systems) finds it a source of much trouble, since letters which were intended to be light will afterwards be mistaken for heavy ones, and vice versa.

The stand from which ink is used should be kept securely corked while not in use, in order to prevent the ink from becoming thick from evaporation or from dust settling in it. The stands used in most offices are, as a rule, "large mouthed arrangements" to which a cover would be a great surprise, and, as a consequence, the contents soon become more like ordinary mud than a writing fluid. An inkstand with a large opening is far more convenient; but, in order to keep the contents in a proper condition, it should be carefully covered when not in use. Of the various kinds of ink which we have used, we have found Thomas' writing fluid to be the best for all purposes whatever, in longhand as well as Shorthand. For a ready, even flow there is none better. If the beginner would, as far as possible, remove all impediments from the way of his becoming a successful reporter, he should give special attention to securing ink which will not make his writing seem the most discouraging part of his work.

XVII. Use a Pencil of Medium Hardness.

Although we would not advise the constant use of a pencil, yet there is no Shorthand writer who will not, at times, be obliged to make use of one. He may break or lose his pen and not have time to secure another, or he may be compelled on unexpected occasions to use paper totally unfit for any kind of a pen; hence he should always be supplied with a few good pencils sharpened ready for use. He should also occasionally write with a pencil so as not to be entirely out of practice when circumstances make it necessary for him to use one. Many reporters use a pencil constantly, preferring it to a pen. If one is able to do better and more satisfactory work with a pencil than with a pen, he certainly ought to use the former.

When selecting a pencil care should be taken not to select one either too hard or too soft. This will depend, to a certain extent, upon the person, and also upon the quality of paper used.

For ordinary use a good quality of uncalendered paper will be found the best for a pencil. Of the various kinds of pencils which we have tried, we have found that the one most suitable for Shorthand is Dixon's "Stenographer." This, we think, will suit most people, though some will find a softer and others a harder quality of the same brand more suitable.

XVIII.   Do Not Fail to be Regular at Recitations.

If nothing more is gained from this suggestion than the habit of attending regularly to your duties, it will have served a worthy purpose.   The habits you form in school will be very likely to cling to you in the practice of your profession, and if you become accustomed to being absent from school you will also find yourself neglecting your employer's work, and, as a result, lose your place.   There is, however, a more immediate disadvantage resulting from being absent from class.   A good teacher, which you are supposed to have, if you have any, will bring up something of importance at each recitation.   By losing some important link in this way, that which is, in fact, a beautifully connected whole becomes disjointed and confused in the mind.   The same result will be brought about by neglecting to thoroughly learn all the little things connected with the study.   In many branches of knowledge a person may neglect many details and not encounter any serious trouble in the further progress of the study, but in Shorthand it is very different.   Here, is allowed no time for reflection.   No chance is given to recall things only vaguely learned.   If you do not have every little point upon the tips of your fingers, failure is in store for you. The only way in which you may be sure of avoiding such a result is to attend promptly every recitation; and not only attend, but make each point presented by the teacher your own.

XIX. Do Not Become Discouraged.

At least three-fourths of those who begin the study of Shorthand get discouraged when about one-fourth of the work is accomplished. They do not stick to it long enough to become accustomed to the study They make mistakes, as beginners in anything do, and not yet being able to appreciate the real beauties of the art, they get discouraged and give up. Young man, stop and think. Although there are thousands and tens of thousands who have begun and then given up the study of Shorthand, yet there are vast numbers who have made a grand success of the work, and men, too, with no more natural ability than many of those who gave it up; the only difference between the classes being, that the one lacked force enough to carry them through, while the other believed that they could do what had been done, and kept at it until they succeeded. There is no study that does not have its difficult parts, and the one who succeeds in these is the one who will not allow every little thing to give him the "blues," while his equally talented brother falls behind and is lost sight of simply because he would not do what he might. A steady application of *will* is a very important factor in considering one's chances of success in the line of Shorthand work.

XX. Do Not Change Systems.

Unless you have begun some system in which you have afterwards found that it is absolutely impossible to become a reporter, do not make a change. I would especially urge this if you have studied a system any length of time. After it has become fixed in the mind that a certain sign stands for a certain sound, it is no easy matter to substitute some other character in its place.

No matter how well you may learn the latter, there will oftentimes be conflict and confusion. Especially will this be the case when you are trying to do rapid writing, since, in trying to do a thing quickly, one naturally does it the way he first learned. Of course, this may, by a great effort, be overcome to a certain extent, yet never completely so. A person will find himself unconsciously confusing the two systems, thus making trouble for himself in translating and his notes absolutely illegible to other reporters of the system which he pretends to write. The habit of representing a word or sound by a certain sign, like any other custom, cannot be laid aside at pleasure, like a garment.

Those people who have used some good system for years and then all at once have found the "ultima thule," in Shorthand, and have become expert reporters in some other system in a few weeks, may be set down as something phenomenal and quite differently constituted from the ordinary mortal. If you are desirous of making some improvement in Shorthand, or wish to test the merits of the various systems, and do not desire to become a rapid writer, you may be justified in making a careful study of the various methods of Shorthand writing; but if your aim is to be a *reporter*, the less you have to do with other systems than the one you have decided to adopt, the better.

It is not advantageous even to adopt contractions from other systems, though they may be more brief, if in any way they conflict with your own. You may not have chosen the best system, but to confuse the one you have, even with a better one, will be very sure to lessen your speed in writing. First, be very careful as to the system you adopt, then stick to it.

XXI. Learn Thoroughly the First Principles.

This is of the utmost importance to the beginner, and yet, as a rule, no part of Shorthand is so much neglected. The first principles seem so easy and simple that students are apt to get the idea that they are not of much consequence. In this they make a very serious mistake. In every system of Shorthand all that follows the first principles is developed from, and dependent upon, them. If these are neglected, as is very often the case, the student, when he comes to the more difficult parts of the study, is almost sure to become confused, get discouraged, and give up. In our experience with persons who have begun the study of Shorthand and made a failure of it, we have, in the large majority of cases, been able to trace their failure to this cause. By not having a thorough knowledge of that part of the art which is the most easy to learn, the whole becomes a complicated and confused mass. No wonder that so many find Shorthand *hard* to learn and make a regular botch of it, when they have not taken the pains to learn the a, b, c's of the art.

The student of Stenography cannot impress too thoroughly upon his mind the elementary principles of Shorthand. As a rule, the extra amount of time spent in thoroughly mastering the elements will be more than saved by the ease and rapidity with which the more difficult parts are acquired.

XXII. Hold Your Pen in That Manner in Which You Can Do the Best and Most Satisfactory Work.

There are teachers who would compel all students to conform to one fixed position. There are others who insist just as strongly on some other position, declaring that there is no success without adopting their particular hobby. But man is not a machine, all the parts of which will fit exactly in the same mould or move about in their spheres with the same harmony. Even though every person had the same style for holding the pen or pencil, yet to confine him to this, with no chance of varying it, would be unreasonable, since it would make the physical strain of writing much greater. A slight shifting of the pen now and then from between the thumb and forefinger to a position between the first and second fingers will be a great relief in steady writing. Again, many find it easier to write with the pen held very nearly perpendicular. A person may compel himself to conform to any particular style of holding the pen and be able to do quite satisfactory work; but unless the style to which he is already accustomed is a very cramped and awkward one, it is better to retain it, since it requires more time to become accustomed to another than would be gained by the change.

There are, it is true, certain general rules to which all should conform, but farther than this nothing can be said. Hold your pen in the manner which is the most natural and easy for you, and so that it will move easily and lightly upon the paper. It will be found that the distinction between the light and shaded letters can be made more readily by holding the pen in a more upright position than it is generally held in writing longhand.

XXIII. Sit at the Table upon Which you are Writing in an Upright and as Easy a Manner as Possible.

The Shorthand writer, as well as the longhand writer, will find it advantageous to cultivate the habit of sitting in an upright position while writing. Unless the left-hand is used, the student will find the right-oblique position the best for steady work. It will also be advantageous to sometimes vary this position to that of a full-front. Such a change will afford a considerable rest to one who is writing steadily. The muscles below the elbow should rest upon the table so as to allow the hand to move freely across the paper. Although the finger movement will be used in most strokes in Shorthand, yet the wrist and full arm movement may occasionally be used to good advantage. The feet should be set squarely on the floor and not drawn up under the chair, as is often done. Young people are very apt to form such a habit, and will find it hard to overcome, yet in the end they will be able to work much more comfortably by assuming a proper position.

XXIV. Hold Your Paper or Note Book Firmly with the Left-Hand.

This can best be done by placing the tips of the fingers of the left-hand upon the edge of the paper at right angles with the right-hand, keeping the thumb against the edge of the paper. By a slight pressure of the fingers, the paper can be held firmly in place, while, with the thumb at the edge of the paper, the page can be readily turned with it as soon as the last line is written. This is a far more important suggestion than it may seem, since but poor work, at best, can be done, unless the paper is firmly held in its place.

XXV. The Learner, as well as the Reporter, Should Use a Good Quality of Paper.

The student can do a hundred per cent. better work with good paper than with the miserable stuff that is for sale at most small book and stationery establishments. The appearance of the work which a student does goes a great way towards encouraging or discouraging him in his efforts. The difference in price of paper will be a small item compared with the real advantage to be gained. Nicely calendered paper should be used in writing with a pen, and the beginner should at first confine himself to one. After he has practiced for some weeks he may then, to good advantage, make use of a pencil. It would be better never to use a pencil at all were it not for the fact that every reporter is occasionally situated so that he is obliged to use one. This being the case, it is quite essential that all reporters become accustomed to writing with a pencil. When using a pencil a good quality of uncalendered paper should be made use of. This will enable one to make a clear distinction between light and shaded letters without much effort, while the writing will not be blurred by the pages rubbing together in handling. The learner will find it convenient to use tablets of paper, of which each leaf may be torn off as soon as used. These should not be destroyed, but laid aside, and afterwards carefully read over.

XXVI.   Do Not Draw Your Shorthand Characters.

The exercises written in Shorthand in most text-books have a tendency to cause students to fall into this habit. The engravings are, as a rule, made with as near an approach to mathematical exactness as it is possible for them to be.   The student, in order to make his work look anything like the illustrations which are given in his text, finds it necessary to make his strokes with a great deal of care, and, as a result, forms the habit of making them very slowly.   Although it is desirable that the student be as nearly correct as possible, and although it is true in most cases that the more perfect the model toward which one is aiming the better he is likely to become, yet a near approach to perfection cannot be made at once.   This is especially true of the beginner in Shorthand who would have his characters exactly like the models in his text, if they are made with mechanical exactness, for in his attempt to closely imitate his model he is sure to form the habit of drawing his letters.   He could not fall into a worse habit, both as regards his speed and the ease and neatness of his work.   The fine penman executes his most beautiful curves and flourishes by rapid and easy strokes.   So in Shorthand the best work can be accomplished in the end by cultivating a free and easy movement.   The work will be more nearly correct, will look much better, and the speed will not be sacrificed.   The reporter is not supposed to have time to draw his characters, and the less that is done of it, even in learning to write, the better.   The writing may not look so well at first, but by patient practice it will, in the end, look far better than though the student had continued to draw out each letter, while the speed will be very much greater.

If you try to make your strokes quickly, and your work is not at first mechanically exact, do not be discouraged, but bear in mind the fact that you can gradually bring your work to approach that point by steady and careful practice.

XXVII. Do Not Make Your Characters Too Large.

There are several reasons why it pays to write a small hand. I do not mean by this a cramped style which is as difficult to write and looks no better than the other extreme, or a large and sprawling style. It takes a great deal more time to write a character twice as long as need be than it does to strike it the proper length. Many Shorthand writers are not aware how much time they lose by making all the characters much larger than is necessary.

To save time is the one thing for which Shorthand is learned, and to spread the characters out over double the necessary amount of paper is but to defeat, in a great measure, the end sought. More time is taken in making larger characters, more time is taken in going back to the beginning of lines, and more time is needed to turn over the larger number of pages. These things, small, very small, in themselves, *count* in the end of weeks or months, and may be saved just as well as not.

Another thing worthy of notice is the amount of paper used. Many reporters use at least twice as much paper as others in writing the same amount of matter. This is another little thing, but which in time will prove to be a very important item. Shorthand written in a small, neat hand also looks much better and more like the work of an artist than does the ordinary scrawl which is adopted by so many stenographers.

XXVIII. Make Your Shorthand Characters Uniform in Length.

Almost every system of Shorthand makes use of the principle of having different lengths for certain characters to indicate certain additional sounds. This is a very important principle in Shorthand, and could not very well be dispensed with. It, however, becomes a very serious stumbling block to many students for the simple reason that the medium sized letters, which are learned first, are not generally made of uniform length. If there were but one length for letters, this would not make so much difference, since the only effect would be to make the writing look uneven. The trouble comes when the same characters are to be made double length or half length, and when so written represent certain additional sounds. If, then, the student has not acquired the habit of writing each class of the characters of a uniform size, he will be sure to get them confused when he comes to reading what he has written. The only way to avoid trouble of this kind is to give particular attention, in the very beginning, to writing the letters of as near a uniform length as possible.

XXIX. In Shorthand No Silent Letters Are Written.

After one has studied the subject of Shorthand a while, and become accustomed to writing by sound, he will have no difficulty at all in distinguishing the silent letters from those which are sounded. At first, however, the student is very apt to be more or less troubled with such letters, and will find himself very often unconsciously inserting many which, upon second thought, he will readily see should not be written. The only way to avoid this, which to the beginner seems a very difficult thing, is to exercise a little care and common sense in the start.

XXX. Make Distinct Angles.

Most students do not give enough attention to making distinct angles between the letters of a word and between different words which are joined. Distinct angles are quite essential to legibility in Shorthand notes. Without something to enable one to distinguish readily where each letter ends and the next begins, the notes will be almost worthless. In using the various ticks especial care should be taken or they will entirely disappear. It is the tendency among students to neglect angularity. This is, no doubt, caused by the fact that many very slight angles may be made quite distinct while writing slowly. The student must take into consideration, however, that only those angles should be formed which can be distinctly made while writing rapidly. As it is not possible for a beginner to always decide just what angles may be made rapidly and at the same time plainly, the only way for him to settle such a matter is to be guided by the experience of those whose opportunities in practice enable them to judge correctly about such things. Our experience has been that students, not having had much practice and not being able to appreciate the practical utility of such forms, oftentimes refuse to adopt them, and accustom themselves to what they suppose to be

3

better outlines. The result is, when they come to use them in reporting, the outlines are found to be unsuitable, and they are obliged to discard them and adopt different forms before they can do satisfactory work.

Although we would not advise students to follow blindly everything a text-book or a teacher may advise, yet in many things the learner may derive a great deal of benefit from the experience of the teacher or author, and save himself from the trouble of having to go through the ordeal of finding out by practice the best form to adopt in each case.

XXXI. At the Beginning of the Study Be Careful About the Slant of Letters.

Unless special attention is given in the beginning of the student's practice he will be very apt to make too little distinction between slanting and upright strokes. Especially is this true in attempting to make perpendicular letters, as it seems almost impossible for most people to make them anywhere near straight up and down. The majority of people are sure to slant the upright letters more or less to the right. As a result, they are almost certain to get them confused with letters intended to slant in that direction.

A good way to overcome this tendency is to use, for a while, paper that is ruled both ways. The upright letters should be struck as nearly parallel as possible with the perpendicular ruling. It will not take a great deal of practice of this kind to enable the student to readily make enough distinction between the different strokes so that there will be no danger of confusing them. Another good plan is to make the perpendicular letters slant a little to the left. But in this, care must be taken not to give them too much slant in that direction, else no advantage will be derived. As the upright letters are the only ones with which students have any trouble, particular attention should be given to them.

XXXII. Learn the Vowels Thoroughly.

Usually there is not one vowel in a thousand written by the Shorthand writer, yet it is quite essential that the student should thoroughly acquaint himself with them. He should do this for two reasons.

First. In the few cases in which it is necessary to insert the vowels, much time will be lost unless the writer is familiar enough with them to insert them quickly. A few moments lost in hesitating as to just where to place a vowel, or the lack of one in an outline which will prove ambiguous without it, will oftentimes cause considerable and serious trouble. For this reason it is important that the student should thoroughly familiarize himself with this part of the study.

Second. In most systems of Shorthand the position of the consonant outline in its relation to the line upon which the writing is done, depends very frequently upon the accented vowel in the word. In this way many vowels are indicated, thus saving the time necessary to insert them. It is for the purpose of indicating them by the position of the outline that a knowledge of the vowels is of chief importance. To be able to give words their proper positions, according to the vowels governing them, it is necessary, not only to learn the vowels as a whole, but also quite essential to learn the different classes governing the different consonant positions.

There are various suggestions given by the different writers who have published text-books on the subject of Shorthand as to the best method to be pursued by the student in familiarizing himself with the vowels, some of which methods are very absurd. The plan which we have adopted, and which has proven very successful, is to give the student, for practice in vocalizing, lists of words which, in ordinary writing, are generally vocalized. By practice of this kind the student does not form the habit of vocalizing words which, in actual practice, should not be vocalized; and what is more, he does become accustomed to vocalizing those words which require it. Lists of words, of which the positions are governed by the vowels, should also be used for practice by the student, as much real advantage may be gained by so doing. The chief difficulty with this plan is that so few text-books contain lists of words of this kind. Students of the Benn Pitman or Graham systems will find that the "Reporting Style of Shorthand" contains many special lists of this kind which will be found very serviceable to any one who will secure the work and make use of them.

XXXIII. Practice a Little Every Day Until the Subject Is Well Understood.

A subject only partly learned is very easily forgotten unless daily attention is given to its study. This is especially true of Shorthand. As Shorthand cannot be used to much advantage until all the principles are learned, a little time each day should be given to the study until it is well understood as a whole. When the connection of the different parts is seen and the art well enough understood to enable one to make practical use of it, it will be valued too highly and too many occasions will occur when it can be used to advantage to admit of the possibility of its ever being forgotten.

The cry that unless Shorthand is constantly practiced it will be entirely forgotten has undoubtedly been caused by that large class of people who have once begun the study, but have lacked the will necessary to succeed. They never have had, at best, more than a vague idea of what Shorthand really is, and, not having enough interest in the subject to keep it constantly before their minds until completed, have given it up, and, as a matter of course, have forgotten what little they ever did know about it. Anything thoroughly understood as a complete whole is never entirely forgotten. But that stage in which it becomes firmly fixed in mind can be reached only by constant and persistent practice, no day being allowed to pass without having made some advancement. By so doing there is no danger of one's interest flagging and of his giving up what would otherwise prove so interesting and profitable.

XXXIV. Until the Principles Are All Learned, Practice Only on Words Embodying Those You Have Mastered, and No Others.

First impressions last longest and are the hardest to remove. The same is true of the manner in which we learn to do things, that which we learn first always coming the most natural to us. This is especially true in writing Shorthand, since a person in trying to do a thing quickly, as is necessary in reporting, is almost certain to go about it in the manner in which he first learned to do it, even though it be a much longer way.

This is one of the great objections to the manner in which most Shorthand text-books are arranged. The most satisfactory way would be to give for practice after each principle introduced an exercise illustrating the use of that principle, and to make use of no other principles except that one and others which have been previously explained. The student should rigidly confine himself to exercises of this kind until all the principles are learned, and he may then be assured that he will form the habit of writing but few words incorrectly, since he would be given no word to write until all the principles entering into its approved outline have been given and explained. The student, by rigidly abstaining from practicing on miscellaneous matter until all the principles of the art and all the word-signs have been learned, ought to have but little difficulty in deciding at once what principles to use in each word, and not to be troubled by long alphabetical outlines continually suggesting themselves to the mind.

XXXV. Keep a List of Word and Phrase-Signs in Your Pocket to Study at Leisure Moments.

At least one-third of the work of learning Shorthand consists in thoroughly mastering the word and phrase-signs. By always having a list of these signs at hand and making it a point to improve now and then your leisure moments which would otherwise be wasted, much of the mechanical part of the work may be accomplished. The author of this little volume was at first discouraged by what seemed an endless task, but by adopting this method the whole was accomplished with apparently no effort whatever. In connection with this, it would be well for the student to have about him some exercise, written several days previous, to translate as occasion offers. This will prove to be a very great help in enabling the student to read readily matter not fresh in mind.

XXXVI. The Student Should Make Use of a Dictionary in all Cases of Doubtful Outlines.

Every good system of Shorthand has a dictionary giving in that system the correct outline or word-sign for all the commonly occurring words in the language. These outlines are, as a rule, those made use of by the best writers of that system, and, in most cases, can be relied upon as being the best form for the word. By a regular use of the dictionary the student will learn far more facile outlines for all difficult words than his own skill will be likely to suggest. Without such help he will learn to write many words by more difficult forms than need be, since, from his inexperience, he would not be likely to think of, or even know, which are really the best. Even if the student had thought of the proper outline for some difficult word, it would afford him considerable satisfaction and encouragement to look up the word and be assured that he had thought of the correct form.

Another great advantage in a constant use of a dictionary is that, in looking up words, many principles and word-signs will be recalled, which otherwise would, in all probability, be entirely forgotten. It is only after reviewing the principles and word-signs over and over again that it is possible to become thoroughly familiar with them. This can be done in no better way than by constant reference to a dictionary. Every reference of this kind will give an illustration of one or more principles, and help to fix them more firmly in mind.

XXXVII. Several Students Should Meet Together Occasionally for Mutual Practice.

Every Shorthand student should, if possible, have a few fellow-students or classmates with whom he may meet occasionally for practice. Much assistance may be derived from mutual suggestions, and by each making it a point to correct the errors he may notice in the other's work. Many a mistake may be pointed out and errors corrected in this way that would otherwise be unnoticed. Another advantage to be gained by this plan is to have some one dictate to you, and to whom you could dictate in return. The student should make it a point to do as little writing as possible by copying, since in practice all Shorthand work is done from dictation. This plan will enable one to increase his speed much more rapidly than could be done by mere copying. The student is also more apt to keep up an interest in the study, if he has one or more classmates. The natural disposition which most young people have, to be as good as their classmates, is a very potent factor, and may be made use of to good advantage in the study of Shorthand.

The difficulty with most people is not what they *can* do but what they *will* do. No one does all that he might.

The most successful man is the one who always places himself in the position in which he will be likely to accomplish the most. Any student might learn history or mathematics at home, yet young people find it necessary to go to some college or university, at a great expense, to learn these subjects. They do this for the simple reason that most men must have a greater incentive to hard study than the mere love of knowledge. In class they feel that to fall behind or totally fail is a disgrace. By sheer force of will the same result might be reached at home, but only a few have a sufficient amount of will-power to enable them to do this. This being the case, other incentives must be sought, and nothing will serve the purpose better than a few determined fellow-students. In the study of Stenography this is especially desirable, and we would advise every one who contemplates learning the art to secure some friend or acquaintance to pursue the course with him. You may be assured that by this method you will do at least fifty per cent. better than by studying alone.

XXXVIII. First, Acquire Accuracy and then, Speed.

Too often students get the false idea that speed is the only thing needful in order to make a first-class reporter. This is a very erroneous notion; for of what value is rapid writing, if it is not done correctly? It is true that a person may, to a certain extent, become accustomed to his own errors, yet he can never read his notes as fluently as if they were properly written, while they will be entirely useless to any one else. It will be far easier to overcome the habit of writing slowly than that of forming outlines incorrectly. In fact the latter is almost impossible to overcome.

Although there seems to be, there is no real conflict between the two. The student ought to be able to form the habit of writing correctly without any danger of retarding the increase of his speed.

XXXIX. Thoroughly Memorize all the Word and Phrase-Signs.

Almost every system of Shorthand is made at least twenty-five per cent. shorter by its word and phrase contractions.

These are, by no means, arbitrary signs, but consist of abbreviations composed of the principal part of the outline of the word or phrase for which they stand. In longhand writing, the words for which we have abbreviations, are, as a rule, words which very seldom occur, as, for example, Rev., Mr., Sept., Pres., etc. In Shorthand, the words for which there are brief signs are those which occur most frequently. Such words as *is, of, or, to, which, for, all, shall, will, he, him, you, your, but, if, in, on, should, our, the,* etc., have in Shorthand contracted forms to represent them.

Although there are but a few hundred of these contractions, yet it is almost impossible to write a sentence of a half-dozen words without using one or more for which there is a sign. This being the case, it becomes very important that you have these signs "upon your fingers' ends." You need not expect to gain any considerable degree of speed without knowing them as well as you know your a, b, c's.

Not only be able to write them correctly at slow dictation, but also know them so well that the sound of the word will cause a picture of the outline to be instantly formed in the mind.

XL.   Leave Blank Lines or a Wide Margin for Corrections after Dictation.

Every Shorthand student will find it advantageous to leave every other line blank, or better, to have his note-book ruled in double columns, and when taking dictation, either in class or privately, to use one column only. After-wards he should go over the work carefully, re-writing the whole in the other column and correcting every mistake he may have made. This will be excellent practice, as it will enable him to see where he is most liable to err in writing. This plan is also very valuable in taking rapid or technical dictation. It gives the reporter room to make corrections or to insert afterwards any part that may have been omit-ted in his endeavor to keep up with the speaker. Any report which is to be got up with a great deal of care, or notes taken at a high rate of speed, should be gone over soon after being taken while it is still fresh in the mind, and all necessary corrections made. This can not be done in a satisfactory manner unless blank lines or a marginal column has been left for that purpose. This plan is adopt-ed by a large number of reporters, especially in doing technical work, and is certainly an excellent one. The marginal column need not, in regular work, be over one-third or one-fourth as wide as the one in which you take your dictation, since, if you are a good reporter, the cases where any corrections are needed will occur only occasionally. The student, however, should have two columns of equal width, and, for some time after beginning regular dictation, should go over all he writes, copying the whole and correcting every mistake that may be found. This should be strictly adhered to by the student for at least a month of daily practice. The real benefit derived from such practice will amply repay the time spent in that way.

XLI. Shorthand Notes are Seldom Punctuated.

In verbatim reporting, and in very many other kinds of work in which a high degree of speed is required, no time is given for the insertion of punctuation marks. By a great many they are not inserted even while writing long-hand, that being left to be attended to afterwards, if done at all. It is, in fact, next to an impossibility for one to always correctly punctuate a sentence until he has heard the whole of it, and, as the reporter oftentimes cannot afford to fall so far behind the speaker, it is plain that he will find it quite impossible to insert the marks in their proper places. Since the words are taken down just as they are spoken, it is easier to insert the marks of punctuation when the transcript is made, for then more time is allowed to attend to it. Generally reporters have no trouble in regard to periods. By some they are regularly inserted. The majority of reporters, however, do not take the trouble to insert even these, but indicate them by leaving a blank space of from one-half to three-fourths of an inch. It is much easier to do this, and it serves the purpose quite as well.

XLII. Do not Phrase Over any Pause or Break of Any Kind in a Sentence.

Shorthand notes, when properly phrased, are, as a rule, more legible than though each word were written separately. In speaking, words are naturally combined into phrases, clauses, or brief sentences, and, in reading, one is enabled to grasp the meaning much more readily, if it is possible to have these combinations of words, which are related to each other either grammatically or rhetorically, set off in some way from what precedes and from what follows. In longhand this is done, to a certain extent, by means of punctuation marks, which are of great assistance in enabling one to grasp the meaning of what is being read. The same advantage may be gained in Shorthand, where, as a rule, no punctuation marks are used, by uniting those parts of a sentence which are naturally related to each other. In order to take advantage of the help which may be secured in this way, care must be taken not to unite words between which there is any grammatical or rhetorical pause. Phrasing, however, cannot be made use of, if the words composing the parts which would naturally be united do not form good angles in joining.

XLIII. Shorthand Notes Must be Legible.

Many of the preceding suggestions bear upon this one point. This suggestion is made with the idea of impressing still more strongly upon the mind the very great importance of giving special attention to all the *little things* connected with Shorthand. It is the neglect of details that, in most cases, causes trouble in translating notes.

Carelessness in shading, in making the proper hooks, in giving the letters the proper slant, in position, and many other things to which reference has already been made, go far toward making the writing illegible. Read over carefully all that has been said concerning these points, and do not allow your writing to be lacking in respect to any of them. It is a common complaint among people who do not know anything about Stenography, and even among many who do pretend to understand it, that Shorthand cannot be read. As a rule, this is caused by the poor writing of those who have not thoroughly learned the art; yet this is not always the case. It frequently occurs that notes which have been taken very accurately cannot be read at all by the writer. There is no other reason for this than that the person has not learned to read Shorthand. There is a vast difference between writing Shorthand and reading it. And here is where a great many fail, simply because they learn only one part of the art and almost entirely ignore the other. Half the work of learning Shorthand consists in acquiring an ability to read without hesitation what has been written. Until one acquires ability in this direction it will make no difference how plainly he may write, his Shorthand will not be legible to him. The extent of one's ability to read notes will determine the extent of their legibility to him, since legibility to each one depends very much upon his familiarity with the characters and the ease with which he can grasp the meanings of the various combinations.

XLIV. Do Not be Afraid to Work.

The successful student does not become such except through patient, determined effort. It makes no difference what line of study he may take up, or how great an amount of natural ability he may have, he must expect to make an effort before he can hope to attain to any measure of success whatever.

Through the misrepresentations so often made by unscrupulous teachers and authors, almost all people have the idea that the study of Shorthand is different from that of any other study, and that the application necessary to fit one for successful reporting is nothing more than a mere pastime. Though this idea is a common one, yet it could not be farther from the truth. To master Shorthand requires *work*, and for some the very hardest kind of work. Until people get over the idea that Shorthand may be "absorbed," we shall be obliged to contend with a large number of incompetent writers. While people have such ideas, it is little wonder that at least one-third of those who claim to be capable of doing good work have never half learned the art.

It does not take a great while for a person of ordinary ability to acquire a practical knowledge of Shorthand, but during his study he must expect to put some honest toil into it. Although it is, for the majority of people, by no means the most difficult study in which one may engage, it is a pastime for none, and the sooner people find this out the better it will be for all concerned.

XLV. Learn Thoroughly the First Principles of Grammar, Punctuation, and Capitalization.

In taking down rapidly the words of another, no time is allowed for giving any attention to matters of this kind. Knowledge of them, however, is absolutely necessary in order to make an acceptable transcript. It will not do to write out a speech or a letter as though it were one long, loose sentence without a pause or a capital in it. Inability to readily capitalize, punctuate, and re-arrange poorly constructed sentences will, and should debar one from the profession. There are, however, thousands of people who have gathered a few vague ideas from some work on Shorthand or attended some school with a "six weeks' course" in the art, and who do not know enough to capitalize the word America or to place an interrogation point after an expression like this: "Does he know anything?", but who think they are competent reporters. It is such that are lowering the standard of the profession, and are either causing or raising the cry of an over-supply. To give satisfaction, the young reporter must be able to carefully correct all obvious grammatical errors made by the speaker, mark off sentences properly, insert the proper marks of punctuation, and capitalize the right words. In order to do this, no small amount of study and practice must be given to the subject.

XLVI. In All Your Practice While Learning the Art, Read, at Least Once, Everything You Write.

This is a part of the student's work which is quite as essential as any other, and yet one more neglected than anything else. It is just as necessary to read Shorthand notes readily as it is to write rapidly. Ability to do this can be attained only by perseverance in that part of the work. We once heard a professor in one of our great universities say that he had, when a boy, learned Shorthand and acquired a very considerable degree of speed in writing, but when he came to translate his first actual work he was totally at sea. Like Dickens, he had either to go back and begin over again or give it up, and he choose the latter. By a few questions we learned that, up to the time he had made his first attempt at reporting, he had never read a single word of what he had written.

Reading and writing are two very distinct operations. In the one, the word suggests the outline, while in the other, it is the reverse, it being necessary for the sign to recall the word for which it stands. As before stated, a person may become expert in writing and at the same time be unable to make any sense at all out of his notes. So, also, might he become a very rapid reader of plain Shorthand notes and not be able to write ten words per minute. A very good illustration of a similar phase of the mind may be found in almost any one of the large numbers who study some foreign language in our colleges. They are able to read French or German or Latin quite fluently, while it is very likely that not one in a hundred can write a single sentence readily and correctly. If we would only bear in mind how long we were in learning to read longhand, we would not hesitate about devoting the comparatively small amount of time necessary to enable us to become expert readers as well as writers of Shorthand.

The only way that the student may be assured he is

4

giving enough attention to this part of the work is to read over, at least once, everything he writes. With this amount of practice he ought, by the time he is able to write one hundred words per minute, to be able to read his notes quite as readily as he does ordinary longhand.

XLVII. Occasionally Read Over Notes Written Several Days Before.

The student can easily find time, and should make it a practice, to read over immediately everything he has written. When he begins actual reporting, however, he will not always be able to do this. In Convention and Law reporting, especially, he will oftentimes be obliged to transcribe notes taken weeks or months or, it may be, years before, and which he has never had an opportunity to read over in the meantime. It also often occurs that an amanuensis is required to go back to his file and make copies of letters or documents of some kind, of which he does not remember the first thing. To be able to do this readily requires more or less practice in reading notes written some time previous, a drill which should not be neglected by the student. In reading what has been written only a few hours before, the memory plays a very important part; but help of this kind is entirely wanting, when it comes to reading old notes. To read readily writing which, to use the common phrase, has become cold, requires the peculiar faculty of being able to grasp the sense where no better clue is given than the context and some of the principal words. The student will find this rather difficult at first, but will be surprised, as he practices more and more, at the ease with which each outline will suggest the proper word.

The reporter's watchword, "Practice," is too often understood only to mean *write*, when it should also mean *read*, as well as to write. And it should not only mean to read each sentence or paragraph as soon as written, and while it can almost be repeated from memory and the notes then to be destroyed, but should mean to go back every now and then and translate notes where the memory will not assist, and where there is nothing upon which to depend but what has actually been written.

XLVIII. Be Able to Go Back and Read Readily Anything You Have Just Written.

It quite frequently happens in dictating that a person forgets the precise statements he has made. This will necessitate his calling for a reading of a portion, or, it may be, of all the paper or letter which he has already expressed.

This is more apt to occur in legal work and in those branches of commercial reporting where exact statements are required. The reporter should be able to go back and read without hesitation any portion desired. Ability to do this can be acquired only by persistent practice. It is, however, quite necessary that the reporter be able to do so, and he should not consider himself competent to fill a position unless he is able to read without hesitation, that which he has just written. Though it may not be possible for him to read fluently matter which has been written at some previous time, in which case the memory does not assist him, yet he ought not to hesitate in reading matter which is perfectly fresh in mind.

XLIX. Correspond in Shorthand with Some Other Student.

There are several advantages to be gained by corresponding in Shorthand with some other student. In the first place, one can keep up a much greater interest in the study. I would especially urge the student to do this, if he is not fortunate enough to have a fellow student with whom he can practice. By corresponding in Shorthand and carefully correcting each other's work, much benefit may be derived; though this plan is not advisable until the student is well through the principles. If an attempt is made to write miscellaneous matter before all the principles are learned, one will be certain to form many words with wrong outlines. Afterwards, when trying to do rapid work, there will be danger of confusing the outline first learned with the correct one. A letter in Shorthand will surely be read, and practice of this kind will aid the student very materially in learning to read his notes readily—a thing which too many are unable to do.

Another advantage which will result from Shorthand correspondence will be the ambition aroused in each to do as well or better than the other. This spirit of emulation, which is a plausible one, will, oftentimes, do more to spur the student on to greater efforts than he is aware of, and in all probability will, in many cases, lead on to a far greater degree of success than one would otherwise attain.

L. Practice on Something You Wish to Learn.

As soon as you are able to write miscellaneous matter, the best plan is to confine yourself, at least a part of the time, to practicing upon something the subject matter of which you wish to make your own. Since it is a good plan to read over all the notes you take at dictation, you can by this means become possessed of many important facts that would otherwise never be learned. A good text-book will have the explanations of the principles embodied, as far as possible, in language suitable for dictation work. This end has been kept constantly in view in the choice of language in these suggestions. The student who is just beginning general dictation work will do well to spend a portion of every dictation exercise in writing some of these suggestions and afterwards translating them and comparing the translation with the original. This, in itself, will be an excellent exercise for the student, while he will also be acquiring, without effort, many valuable points which will never come amiss to him, both in studying and practicing the art.

LI. Keep Cool.

If there is one thing that needs emphasizing more than another of a reporter's qualifications, it is to *keep cool*.

Shorthand needs too much attention to be written properly unless one is perfectly calm. There are times in every reporter's career, even if he is only an amanuensis, which will require all the nerve that he can control to enable him to "get it all down."

To acquire the ability to keep cool under all circumstances is, for most people, by no means an easy task. It is, in fact, almost an impossibility for some. Confining ourselves within the limit of Shorthand, there is no better way to enable the reporter to be deliberate, under all circumstances, than a thorough preparation for the work, such a preparation as will inspire a confidence that you are equal to the task before you. This, with a firm determination that you will succeed, will go far towards making you deliberate and insuring your success. Always bear in mind that a slow writer with a cool head will accomplish far more than a much more rapid reporter who cannot control himself, but gets nervous at every little thing that occurs out of the regular course of events.

LII. Educate the Eye and Ear, as well as the Hand.

The eye and the ear need training quite as well as the hand. There is little or no danger that the hand will not receive enough attention, since no practice can be done without its use. This is too often considered all that is necessary. Many students get the idea that the chief requisite is to get the pencil over the paper rapidly. The proper cultivation of the ear, especially, is neglected. The reporter's work is done almost exclusively by writing from another's speaking. To do this well, the ear and hand must be trained to act together. It is just as necessary that the ear be trained to catch every sound as it is that the fingers be able to form the outlines rapidly. The ear can be trained in no better way than by careful practice in writing at dictation. In order to become accustomed to different voices and different styles of dictation, it is well to have different ones dictate or read to you.

The eye should be so trained as to recognize forms at once, even though they are not mechanically exact. The best way to accomplish this is to *read* Shorthand. Read over all your own notes, and as much as you can of others' writing.

To be an expert reporter these two faculties should be so well trained that one may, without effort, catch every word of a speaker, and unconsciously form in the mind the outline which represents it. One can do this perfectly only after years of practice, and it can never be done satisfactorily at all unless the student is careful in the very beginning.

LIII. Form the Habit of Picturing in Your Mind the Outlines of Words You Hear in Conversation or See in Reading.

Most students will find this an easy and, at the same time, a very profitable habit to acquire. Many students experience considerable trouble in training the mind to act rapidly in recalling the proper outlines for words. They know the outline well enough and can execute it rapidly when once they are able to recall it, but too often they have to stop and think what it is. The only way to attain ability to do this readily is by practice. Of all the qualifications necessary for a reporter, that of recalling outlines readily is, without doubt, one of the most difficult to acquire; yet by a little effort towards forming the habit of recalling the outlines of words which are heard and read, one will soon find it easy to write without hesitation the outline for any word that may occur. The student, however, should not suppose that ability to recall words quickly is *all* that is necessary to enable him to write rapidly. The fingers must also be trained to move rapidly, and in harmony with the power of recalling the characters. Hence, that kind of drill which will bring both into action at once, and train them to act harmoniously should not be neglected.

LIV. Write Your Shorthand Characters Near Each Other.

There are three important points to be gained by making use of this suggestion. In the first place, time is saved. It takes as long again to move a quarter of an inch as it does to move an eighth, and to save half the time generally taken by most Shorthand writers who separate their characters quite widely will be found to considerably increase one's speed. A second advantage, though apparently a trifling one, is the saving of paper, which may be made by writing the signs much nearer to each other than most reporters do. It is undoubtedly true that a great many reporters leave nearly, if not quite, as much blank space between the characters as is occupied by the outlines themselves. With the reporter who is doing a large amount of writing this will prove to be no small item. Besides, it makes the work look more compact and connected than if each word or phrase stood out as though it were an isolated or disjoined part. A third advantage to be urged in favor of writing the characters closely together is that it enables the writer to indicate more readily by a blank space a full pause or any important break in the sentence. It would be hard to thus indicate these unless the words were written reasonably close together.

LV. Copy Several Times All the Phrases Given in the Phrase Book.

Every system of Shorthand has or should have a book of phrases as well as a dictionary. Much time may be saved and in many places the sense made plainer by properly joining the words into phrases. All the words of short sentences even may be joined, if a good angle occurs at each juncture. The student from his inexperience cannot, of course, always know when it is best to join words, and when not to join them. In fact he will find that learning to *phrase* is one of the most difficult things he will meet with in his endeavor to become a reporter.

The beginner is very apt to phrase too much. He is liable to join words when the angle between them is very slight. This may be done while writing slowly, since a slight angle could then be made distinct, but the student must bear in mind that only those words should be united which may readily be joined, and between which the angles are such that they may be easily and distinctly made while writing rapidly. He can learn this only by gaining his information from those who have had experience, or from some work embodying the results of the experience of some practical reporter, since the student himself can have had no chance to gain such information from his own practice.

A good phrase book will contain all the commonly occurring phrases which are easily and readily formed while writing at a high rate of speed. By writing them ten or fifteen times, the student will find himself almost unconsciously overcoming what before seemed an insurmountable obstacle.

LVI. Learn to Keep Long Sentences in Mind.

With the reporter ability in this direction is quite essential to success, not only in taking notes but also in making transcripts of the same.

Although it is advisable for the reporter to closely follow the speaker, yet he should be able to occasionally fall considerably behind, and at the same time not lose a word that is uttered. Unless the student has acquired ability to do this, he will be sure to fail when an unexpected spurt is made by the speaker. He will have ample opportunity to catch up during the pause which a speaker always makes after every flight in his delivery.

Ability to retain long sentences in mind will also prove of advantage in transcribing, since it will save a vast amount of time in referring back and forth from the copy to the work. A person in copying should be able to retain at least twenty-five or thirty words in his mind at a time. By being able to do this, work may be done much more rapidly.

One's ability in this direction will depend, to a great extent, upon his practice and the kind of matter to be copied. Much improvement, however, may be made by constant and patient endeavor. Persons who, at first, are not able to retain half a dozen simple words can easily increase their ability at least fourfold.

LVII.   Reporters Often Contract Long Outlines.

In writing words with long outlines or terms composed of several words which occur quite frequently in a long report or in a business in which one is engaged, the reporter will find it greatly to his advantage to abbreviate the outlines to a considerable extent. This would not do, if they occurred only rarely, as very little and often times no help at all could be derived from the context in reading; but in matter in which they appear scores of times no trouble need be caused by contracting them very considerably every time they occur.

In various kinds of law reporting, especially, certain long legal terms occur very frequently. The outline for these should be contracted by the reporter. Every kind of business, in fact, has a large number of words and phrases peculiar to itself and for which the reporter can easily form contractions. It may seem strange to some that word-signs for such words are not given in works on Shorthand. This is not advisable, for the reason that there has come to be such a great variety of work for reporters that, if each were to learn all the special contractions used in every kind of business, he would be obliged to tax his memory with a very large list of signs which, in practice, he would never have occasion to use.

With the present confusion of so many systems we can see no better plan than for each Stenographer to adopt brief outlines for those words and expressions which are of most frequent occurrence in the line of work in which he is engaged. Care should, of course, be taken to adopt only those forms which are both brief and easily written and at the same time full enough to save trouble in reading them.

LVIII. Do Not Allow the Pen to Stop Between the Different Parts of a Word or Different Words of a Phrase.

Students are apt to fall into the habit of making a full stop at angles and even between letters where there is no angle at all. Where there is an acute angle to be formed a stop must, of course, be made, yet it need not be a perceptible one. . If there is no angle at all and the parts are joined by a curved stroke, no pause whatever should be made. Much time is lost by pauses of this kind, and, unless the student is careful, he will allow this habit, which he necessarily formed in the very beginning of his practice, to become so strong that it will be hard to overcome.

LIX. Always Have the One Who Dictates to You Speak a Little Faster Than You Can Write.

If nothing of this kind is done to urge you to greater efforts, you can not expect to increase your speed very rapidly. The teacher who understands his business will, by a regular increase in his rate of dictation, gradually lead his pupil up to a speed that will enable him to do practical work. This, however, must be done slowly. Speed in Shorthand is not acquired by long and rapid strides. It is uphill work, and proficiency can be attained only by taking one small step at a time until the utmost limit is reached.

LX. Learn to Operate the Type-Writer.

Shorthand and type-writing are twin brothers. I might almost say Siamese twins. Until within the last few years it was not considered a necessary qualification for a reporter to understand the use of the type-writer. During late years, however, writing machines have been so greatly improved that by their use much time may be saved, both in writing and reading. As a result, the majority of places where a large amount of writing is done, and especially where a Stenographer is employed, the type-writer is also used. By the use of the writing machine, notes may be transcribed in at least one-half the time required in long-hand, and in a far more legible manner. Another very great advantage in the use of the type-writer is that one may make two or more copies at the same time without extra work. One can also write much longer without tiring the muscles of the hand as is done in writing long-hand, since there is more variation in the movement, and both hands are used. Pen paralysis is destined to become a thing of the past, and writing will come to be, in a great measure, a pastime instead of the drudgery it is with the pen.

Before beginning to practice upon the type-writer the student should have a thorough explanation of the machine made to him by some experienced operator, or make a thorough study of it, guided by some manual of instruction.

Speed depends, to a great extent, upon a systematic manipulation of the keys, and unless care is taken, especially in the beginning, one will become accustomed to make many moves which will retard rather than facilitate the work. It may be monotonous at first, yet it is very essential that the beginner adhere, as nearly as possible, to some regular system of practice until he can follow it without conscious effort.

LXI. Learn to Take Care of the Type-Writer.

There is, probably, not more than one place in fifty where Stenography is made use of in which the reporter is not only expected to know how to operate the type-writer, but is also supposed to understand how to take care of the machine. For one who thoroughly understands the machine keeping it in good running order is no task at all. The later styles of type-writers are so simple that after a few hours' examination, any person ought to understand the workings of all its parts well enough to run it with the least possible wear. This, however, is far from being the case. So much so, that one would suppose the ordinary type-written letters sent out by the majority of our large business houses were written on a machine which had been used for an age, when, in all probability, six months would include the full extent of its usage; yet a good type-writer properly taken care of ought to do five hours' work or more every day for ten years.

Every type-writer company, in sending out its machines, sends with each one a book of instructions. This is generally very explicit in its directions, and any one who will give these a little careful study ought to have no trouble in keeping his instrument in order. The great trouble is that the majority of operators have never seen one of these books. Another trouble arises from the fact that very few ever pay the least attention to the mechanism of their machines. It does not require a mechanical genius to find the difficulty when something gets out of order, nor does it take an expert to regulate all the different parts; but it does require that a little common sense be used, a thing which is too seldom done by a great many so-called type-writer operators.

The use of the type-writer would be greatly increased were it not for the discredit cast upon it by the work of so many poor operators. It is needless to say that the type-writer is a really excellent machine, and that it will, some day, supersede the use of the pen; but it can never be done until a higher standard of work is demanded. This point cannot be reached until operators better understand the machine they operate, and take more pride in their work.

LXII. Practice on the Kind of Business in Which You Expect to Engage.

What we mean by this suggestion is to familiarize yourself, as far as possible, with the nature and especially the duties connected with the business upon which you intend to enter. For instance, suppose you intend to act as an amanuensis for some wholesale book and publishing house, you will find that the more you know of the book trade, and especially the correspondence connected therewith, the easier it will be for you to secure a position, and to fill it satisfactorily after you have secured it.

Of course there will be a great deal you cannot learn until you are actually engaged in the work, yet a few general ideas of a business will give a person more confidence in himself than he would otherwise have, and also enable him to understand many other things much more readily than he otherwise would.

If possible, the student should secure letters or copies of letters relating to the business in which he expects to engage, and by their help familiarize himself, as far as may be, with the technical terms and peculiarities of that particular kind of work.

The student who is fitting himself for general work cannot, of course, profit much by this suggestion, and he will find his work proportionally harder in the beginning.

LXIII. The Amanuensis May Adopt, to Good Advantage, Contracted Forms for a Large Number of Words and Expressions of Frequent Occurrence in His Special Work.

Every kind of profession or business has a large number of words and phrases peculiar to it. Outside of the range of these particular branches these words are very seldom used. Hence it is not advisable for the student to spend time in learning a long list of abbreviations, a large per cent. of which are made use of only in special lines of work. The better plan is for the student to learn only the signs for the most commonly occurring words and phrases. Then, when he has decided to engage in any particular kind of business, or, better, after he has had opportunity to gain some experience in it, he will find it an easy matter to contract the outlines for the words and phrases peculiar to that profession or business, and for the stereotyped expressions to which his employer is particularly addicted.

Most reporters devise contractions for such terms and expressions, and find them very helpful in expediting their work and in no way affecting the legibility of their notes.

LXIV. Do Some Practical Work for Some Business Man.

The best kind of practice the student can have, after he has learned the principles, is that which approaches most nearly to the kind of work he will be obliged to do in actual reporting. Business men, in fact, prefer those who have had some practical experience, and in order to be able to satisfy them that you are not a mere beginner, you should secure some actual practice just for the experience it will give. Go to some business man who has more or less correspondence and offer to take all his letters for a while without wages. You can well afford to do this. In the first place, you would be fitting yourself for the actual work in the most thorough and practical manner possible. If your work is satisfactory, and you ought not to expect a paying position until it is, it would be much easier to secure a situation and to fill it acceptably than you might otherwise hope to do. Another advantage that often arises from such a course is in causing the man for whom you work to learn to appreciate the advantages of Shorthand, and, in this way, cause a demand for your own employment, or for that of some other Shorthand writer.

LXV. A Knowledge of Book-Keeping and Business Forms is Often Very Serviceable to the Amanuensis.

There are many places where the services of a Stenographer are required, although there is not enough work in that line to keep one constantly employed. In cases of this kind an amanuensis is usually required to assist in keeping the books, filling out orders, checking bills, or something of a similar nature.

Situations of this kind are, of late, becoming very common. Heretofore, those whose business was not extensive enough to enable them to give a Stenographer steady employment have not made use of such assistance at all. They are, however, beginning to realize that they can gain the advantage of such help by employing a reporter who can also assist at other things when not engaged in stenographic work.

5

This is opening for Stenographers a new field which will, before many years, more than double the demand for Shorthand writers. In order to occupy this field, the reporter must qualify himself for the other duties which will necessarily be coupled with it.

LXVI. Do Not Disturb the One Dictating.

This suggestion, it is plain, will apply more particularly to those engaged in amanuensis work.

In composing letters the dictator is governed by the same feeling which controls one while conversing with another. He talks as if the party to whom he is writing were actually present, and he were speaking to him, answering some important question, or making some proposition. This being the case, any interruption will be just as disagreeable as though he were in actual conversation with the correspondent himself.

It also requires considerable mental effort to indite letters and other matter rapidly and correctly, and any unnecessary interruption, either by lack of speed, being nervous, or by asking questions, will tend to confuse the dictator and make him impatient. In order to give satisfaction, such things must be scrupulously avoided.

The amanuensis should also hold himself in readiness to begin writing at the very instant his employer begins to dictate. The necessity of so doing is caused by the fact that most people who have amanuenses are people who do not understand Shorthand, and who cannot realize that it is possible for the reporter to get all they say unless he begins to write at the very moment the dictating commences. Although it may be perfectly safe to fall fifteen or twenty words behind the speaker, still, in most cases, much hesitation and nervousness on the part of the dictator may be avoided by being ready to take, as soon as uttered, the very first word, both at the beginning of letters and after each pause made by the one dictating.

LXVII. In Doing Amanuensis Work, if Any Important Statement Is Not Distinctly Heard, Call for Its Repetition.

This may seem to be in contradiction to the preceding suggestion. This, however, is not the case. It would hardly be considered any more of an interruption to ask the dictator to repeat a statement that had not been distinctly heard than it would be for one person to ask another to repeat something which, in ordinary conversation, he had not heard or the meaning of which he had not understood.

If it is only a matter of minor importance that is not exactly understood, it is better to let it pass until the end is reached, and then ask for its repetition. Blank space should be left, however, to insert anything that may have been lost. It would also be well to make some sign on the margin to indicate where the omission was made or otherwise in looking for it; the blank may be taken simply for a pause or change in the subject, and thus be overlooked.

LXVIII. The Amanuensis Should Leave a Wide Margin so as to Have Room to Make Any Insertions Which the Dictator May Afterwards Desire.

It very often occurs, especially in dictating legal and other technical matter, that the dictator wishes to go back and insert some clause, modify some statement, or give a more complete explanation of some difficult point. Unless a margin is left beside the notes, it will be necessary to make a note of the changes at the close of the dictation. When placed at the end it frequently occurs in transcribing that they are forgotten until it is too late to write them in their proper places. Some amanuenses always place anything of this kind at the end, and then insert some sign in the notes where the insertion is to be made. This is just as good a plan only it requires more time and is apt to be misunderstood by others who may have occasion to refer to the notes at some future time.

LXIX. Keep a List of the Full Names and Postoffice Addresses of All Regular Correspondents.

By keeping a list of this kind, the full name and address need not be written out at the beginning of each Shorthand letter. This will avoid the necessity of keeping one's employer waiting while the names are being written, and also save him the trouble of repeating before each letter the full name and address of the party to whom he is writing. The date, with the full name and address, may be filled in afterwards. This may seem to some like a small matter, but when one has to write a hundred or a hundred and fifty short, pointed business letters at a single take, he will find that nearly as much time will be occupied in writing out the full heading for each letter as is necessary to write the whole body of the letter in Shorthand. Even if the Stenographer does not care to keep a list of the principal correspondents, he need not always write the name in full when taking the letters, as he will be able, after a little practice, to fill out most of them from memory. All those who cannot safely trust their memory to do this should be sure to keep a full list of the regular correspondents.

LXX. Keep Your Own Counsel.

The Stenographer, like everybody else, must, in a certain sense, be a machine. This arises from the fact that in many cases confidential matter of the gravest importance is often dictated to him, and unless he exerts the utmost care, he will be apt, inadvertently it may be, to betray a knowledge of his employer's affairs to those who would take advantage of it. Again, it frequently occurs in some kinds of business that the Stenographer is approached for the special purpose of persuading him to make known his employer's intentions or plans. Attempts may even be made to bribe him in order to secure the desired information. Aside from the moral phase of the question, the Stenographer can, by no means, afford to betray his employer's secrets to others. Once let it be proven that he has done such a thing and his prospects as a reporter will be ruined.

Morally it is wrong, and financially it is a losing investment. If you find that you have a tendency to speak of things pertaining to your work to those not connected with the business, it would be well to form the habit of rigidly refusing to speak of your employer's affairs at all. By so doing there is no risk of being surprised into statements which may afterwards be regretted.

LXXI. Perform Your Work to Suit Your Employer.

Your employer pays you for your services, and they should therefore be rendered in a way agreeable to his wishes. Too often beginners are informed, soon after taking a position, that their services are no longer required, simply because they have persisted in doing things as they themselves thought best, when they were well aware that their employer had been in the habit of doing or having the same things done in another way. Although you may be sure that your methods are better, if he does not think so, that should end the matter.

In most matters relating to the Shorthand part of the business, employers leave all to the management of their amanuenses. They do, however, generally have some regular forms which they have followed for years; as, for example, they have a certain plan of filing away their letters, and do not wish to disarrange their business by changing, even though some new plan might be a little better. The amanuensis should be perfectly willing to adapt himself to such arrangement. In case no particular forms have been made use of, and the employer is willing that the reporter introduce plans of his own, there can be no objection to his doing so.

LXXII. Take an Interest in Your Employer's Affairs.

This will apply in general to those engaged in any kind of business, but certainly applies with special force to the amanuensis reporter. As such, the reporter knows more about his employer's business than any other person in his service. He cannot help knowing all about many of his employer's intentions and plans. Being thus situated he ought to manifest an interest in the business. Knowing so much about the business, it can scarcely be that he will not have many confidences trusted to him. It will also very frequently happen that the reporter will learn of things greatly to the interest of his employer. When anything of this kind occurs he should feel it his duty to give him the benefit of such knowledge. The amanuensis may, in this way, be able to give timely warning against some course that might occasion serious loss, or, at another time, he may gain some information by which his employer might greatly profit. Anything of this kind will be duly appreciated, and will be almost sure to result in the promotion of employees who take the trouble to so interest themselves.

LXXIII. Secure a Seat in Front of and as Near the Speaker as Possible.

In amanuensis work the reporter generally performs his duties in the private office of his employer where there is not likely to be anything to disturb or interrupt. Reporting in public, however, is quite different, and to avoid the danger of missing any part of the proceedings, the reporter should make it a point to secure a suitable location. As a rule, it will be found that a position immediately in front of the speaker will be most suitable. When it is expected that reports are to be made, tables are generally furnished, and placed in the most convenient position for the use of reporters.

Never try to write behind the speaker, if any other place at all can be secured. The gallery should be avoided unless it is known to be suitable for the purpose. In making reports of conventions, mass meetings, etc., a seat at the same table with the secretary is the most suitable place. as he generally knows the names of all who take part, and is also able to give other information necessary to a full report.

The court reporter will be more likely to hear every word by being seated between the judge and jury. They are generally seated near each other, and as everything of importance is intended for either one or the other or both, the reporter will not, by being between them, be apt to miss anything that is said.

LXXIV. Make a Note of Everything That Takes Place as well as What Is Said.

To make a report intelligible to readers, it very often becomes necessary to explain certain things which occurred during the progress of the meeting of which a report is being made. Something may happen to call forth from the speaker an expression in no way related to the subject under discussion, or, it may be, cause him to entirely change the course of his remarks. Unless some explanation is made to show the reason for this, the reporter would do an injustice to the speaker. A certain noted lecturer, referring to the fine arts, made the following remark while addressing an audience in one of our large cities : "What shall I say of the composition of Mozart?—Such music is enough to try the patience of the gods.—The tender pathos, the soul stirring strains, the sweet harmony, of the great composers have done more to make mankind better, than all the cold philosophy of the ages." The next morning the news was spread abroad that Mr. ———— had publicly ridiculed one of the great masters, while, at the same time, pretending to be a patron of classical music. A word of explanation by the reporter would have shown that the disparaging remark had nothing whatever to do with the discourse, but was caused by a brass band, in the immediate neighborhood, bursting out at that very moment, in a most indescribable discord of harsh sounds.

In court reporting it is quite necessary, often times, to insert explanatory notes in order to explain certain statements made by the witnesses. Thus, if the question were asked, "How far were you standing from Mr. Mandel when he was struck?" and the answer should be, "About as far as from here to the stove," it would be necessary for the reporter to insert in parenthesis a statement giving, as nearly as possible, the distance indicated.

From what has been said any one will readily see the bearing of this suggestion. This should enable one to avoid the danger of difficulty arising from lack of any needed explanation.

LXXV. The First Time a Proper Name Occurs Write It in Longhand.

This suggestion should be followed whenever practicable, since the stenographic outline does not indicate the spelling, and hence, when it comes to transcribing, many names, if written in Shorthand only, would be improperly spelled. Once writing the name in longhand will, however, be sufficient for each report, since this gives the spelling, after which it is perfectly safe to write it in Shorthand. When it is impossible to write out the word, the next best thing to do is to carefully vocalize it. This should always be done, especially when two or more names have the same outlines, as in the case of John, Jane and Jean. The only way these names could be distinguished in most systems of Shorthand is to vocalize them. It is customary, among most Shorthand reporters, not to take the trouble to underscore proper names which are thus vocalized.

LXXVI. The Field of Court Reporting or of the Law Amanuensis Offers the Most Excellent Opportunities to Those Who Contemplate Entering the Legal Profession.

There is no better school for the student of law than that of court reporting. His duties, as such, bring him constantly in contact with judges and skilled practitioners. In every trial which he reports, he sees applied in practice the principles which he has learned from books, and has them impressed upon his mind in a manner which no amount of reading or study would do. His opportunities to become well versed in the law of evidence, a most important branch of the legal profession, are unsurpassed. The forms and methods of procedure are also important, and no better place can be found than the reporter has for becoming familiar with them.

As an amanuensis in a good law office, one may derive almost as much profit as is gained by the court reporter. The fact that one is able to write Shorthand will also prove a very potent factor in securing a preference over another who cannot report. Many a young man has, by the help of Shorthand, been able to secure a good position in some

large law office, where otherwise he would have had no
show at all.

LXXVII. The Court Reporter Should Understand Thoroughly the Nature of the More Ordinary Rulings, Exceptions, and Objections Made Use of in Court Procedure, so as to Be Able to Make Proper Record of Them.*

Next in importance to the evidence itself is the record-
ing of objections, which are made from time to time to its
introduction, or to any proceeding which either party may
consider illegal. The grounds upon which such objections
are based should be noted by the reporter, and should they
not be stated specifically, the counsel's argument in presenting the matter to the court should be taken down.
When an objection is decided, the exception, if any, taken
by the party overruled, should also be recorded.

Exceptions are also taken to the decisions of the court
in sustaining or overruling various motions submitted in
the course of the trial, and a minute should be made of
them by the reporter.

In reporting depositions, objections are recorded and
testimony taken subject thereto, no rulings being made, or
exceptions taken at the time.

A law report should be, as nearly as possible, a photo-
graph of all the proceedings had. Hence it becomes the
reporter's duty to make a minute of every transaction
which has a bearing on the case.

---

* NOTE.—This, with Suggestion 78, were, with the consent of the author, taken
from the "Reporting Style of Shorthand."

LXXVIII. All Exhibits Introduced in Court as Part of the Evidence Should Be Carefully Marked in the Order in Which They Are Produced.

Written documents, as deeds, notes, contracts, mortgages, letters, depositions, etc., are frequently produced in court, and make a part of the evidence. For the purpose of identification, and convenience in making references, the same should, at the time, be marked by the reporter as exhibit "A," "B," etc., according to the order in which they are introduced. The paper should have upon it, besides the index letter, the initials of the parties to the suit. This prevents ambiguity in the cases where the same document has already been marked with a different letter as an exhibit in another case.

As part of evidence, also, knives, rings, keys, photographs, or any articles whatever which it may be important for the court or jury to examine are from time to time introduced. These may be marked by firmly attaching a written card to them.

The reporter should be careful to identify, as an exhibit, every article or document offered by either party, whether or not the same is actually admitted in evidence by the court, since rejected exhibits are necessary to complete the appellant's bill of exceptions.

Half the value of a law report is lost by not having it properly indexed. The paper used should be accurately paged, and each separate book or manuscript numbered in the order used.

Reference is frequently made, and the reporter ordered to read parts of testimony taken days, or even weeks, previous. This can be done only by means of a running index, which is kept making from hour to hour, just as the proceedings take place. This should give the day and date of each session of court, the name of each witness, and the page where his testimony and cross-examination begins.

LXXIX. In Reporting for Newspapers, Full Notes Should Always Be Taken, Though Only a Condensed Report May Be Required.

Nowadays only brief synopses of reports are printed. These may be prepared much more satisfactorily when done at leisure and from full Stenographic reports. For this reason Shorthand reporters are given the preference on all our metropolitan journals. They do not, as a rule, furnish longer reports, but the fact that they have more opportunity to deliberate upon the matter enables them to use better judgment in deciding just what portions should be made use of and what should be rejected. As a result they are enabled to furnish much more acceptable reports. They also have full notes in case any contingency arises in which a full account is desired.

The newspaper reporter should also be especially well skilled in reading Stenographic notes, since reports must often be taken with a lead pencil on unruled paper, and not unfrequently when the writer is standing. It also very often occurs that reports must be written out very rapidly in order to have them ready for the next issue of the paper. No time is allowed on such occasions for puzzling over notes. The newspaper reporter, if he would make a success of his calling, must be able to read, without meeting with too many difficult points, notes taken rapidly and under all circumstances.

LXXX. In Making Reports of Public Meetings, Conventions. Etc., Where Speeches Are Made by a Number of Persons, Be Careful to Make Note of Each Speaker's Name.

The reporter can best do this by securing a seat near the secretary, who, as a rule, is supposed to know the names of all who take part. If, in reporting the proceedings of a convention of some organized body, it is not possible to learn the names of all who participate, the remarks made by each speaker whose name is unknown should be placed under the head of "A Member."

The president and secretary are generally designated by their official titles and their names not repeated after being given at the beginning of the report. It is also a wise plan to get a list of the names of all the members of organized bodies so as to be able to properly spell each name in making out the report for publication. Such a list may always be obtained from the secretary.

LXXXI. In Convention Reporting, Note Carefully All Motions and Resolutions Except Those in Writing, Also Amendments Thereto, and Remarks and Decisions Thereupon.

In making out reports of all kinds of public meetings it is often the case that much of their real value depends upon matters of this kind. Since most of the regular speeches are generally written before being delivered, the greater part of the reporter's duties will be to record the remarks made upon them and the unwritten motions and resolutions and discussions which they call forth.

In order to succeed in this, several special qualifications are necessary. A keen and cultivated sense of hearing is indispensable, since a writer is often required to take down rapidly the remarks of different members located in various parts of a large assembly, and who sometimes follow one another in quick succession. In convention reporting more judgment, editorial ability, and a previous knowledge of the matter in hand are needed. A thorough understanding of parliamentary rules and the customs of deliberative assemblies is also necessary to satisfactory work in this line.

The best way to properly fit one's self for work of this kind is to serve for awhile as an assistant to some experienced reporter, from whom many things may be learned which cannot be acquired in any other way.

LXXXII. In Speech Reporting, Good Sight and Hearing, as well as Keen Observation and Good Expression, Are Necessary.

Under the general head of speech reporting is included the various kinds of public addresses, religious debates, sermons, etc. In order to make a success in this field something more than that which may be gained by study is demanded. The natural gifts of good sight and hearing are indispensable. Keen observation is another essential, and with this must be coupled force in expression.

Good sight is necessary, since it very often occurs that the eyes will have to endure a long and continuous strain.

Also, in transcribing, the sight is often tried to its utmost extent. This is especially true when pencil notes are to be read, since the closest scrutiny must be made of almost every word in copying notes of this kind, and unless the eyes are strong they will soon fail.

One must also be able to hear well enough to catch distinctly everything uttered by the speaker. Any defect in this respect will totally unfit the reporter for work of this kind, and it is useless to try to substitute any other qualification in its place.

The speech reporter must also be continually on the alert in order to understand not only what is said but also the relation of the different points made by the speaker. Unless he is able to do this, when he comes to make an abstract of what he has written, as he will often be called upon to do, he will be apt to leave out many important matters, and include some things which ought to be omitted.

LXXXIII. Besides Speed the Speech Reporter Must Possess a Fair Knowledge of the English Language, History, and the Current Events of the Day.

Though all of these are important, the latter is especially so. Persons of an enthusiastic temperament, who are fully awake to the importance of current changes, and interested in the living political, religious, and socialistic issues of the day are far the best fitted for reporting public speeches, for these relate almost constantly to such matters. The reporter must also know something of history in order to understand many things which he will be called upon to report, and where he will be sure to fail without such knowledge. He must understand the English language so that he may be able to write out his reports correctly.

With a speed of from one hundred and fifty to one hundred and seventy-five words per minute, taken in connection with enough general information to understand what he is reporting and to transcribe it in a clear and concise manner, and with sufficient judgment to condense when it is required, without omitting any of the salient points, the reporter will be prepared to enter a field, the educational advantages of which are indeed vast, and in which he will find every opportunity to prepare himself for a higher professional life.

LXXXIV. Every Stenographer Should Prepare Himself to Teach Shorthand.

The demand which is fast becoming universal for instruction in this art, and the lack of those who are prepared to teach, make it possible for almost every reporter who has any ability at all in this direction to devote his spare time in a very profitable way.

The qualifications necessary for success in teaching are a good general education, a thorough and accurate knowledge of the theory, power of expression, and an interest in the work. The division of the work is two-fold, the first being that of instruction in the theory; the second, that of the practical application of the art. It is not indispensable that the teacher understand anything more than the theory in order to do satisfactory work in teaching the mere principles of the art. To impart a practical knowledge of the reporting business, however, it is necessary

6

that the teacher should not only understand the theory; but that he should also be an adept in, at least, some one branch of the reportorial calling.

The rapidly increasing demand for Shorthand Amanuenses, the large number who wish to acquire a knowledge of the art for their own private use, and the fact that it has lately been introduced into the public schools in many of our large cities, make it possible for a large number to find profitable employment by devoting a part of their time to teaching.

Apart from the text used, the teacher will be able to derive much help in his work from the various suggestions in this little volume. A careful study of these will give all the special preparation necessary to enable one to do very satisfactory work as a teacher.

LXXXV. When You Are Prepared for a Situation Do Not Sit Down and Wait for One to Come to You.

There are three ways, any one of which the young reporter may adopt, to secure a position.

In the first place, he may sit down and wait for one to seek him out. This is liable to prove rather monotonous. We have known reporters to be almost compelled to take positions which were offered them. Such cases, however, are far from being the rule.

Another plan is to depend upon some one else to assist him. It may be some friend or some bureau on which he places his dependence. These, at best, are liable to fail him. Friends are rare, indeed, who do not consult their own interests first and will only remember others after they have secured all they can for themselves.

A third plan is for the young reporter to be a man, and to depend upon himself, to give people who are likely to need the services of a Stenographer to understand that he is prepared for this kind of work, that he is willing to do the very best he can, and is determined to succeed. Such a spirit will win confidence and respect and assure the possessor of an early opportunity to test his ability, There are plenty of places waiting for some energetic man or woman to push into them and to make a success in them.

LXXXVI. Always Be on Time.

There is no other one thing that will do more towards commending a person to the favor of people than promptness in attending to one's duties. This is the case in every kind of business, but it is especially true of the reporter. In most occupations in which a person is serving another, he may frequently neglect it by tardiness and no one sustain any serious loss. With the Stenographer, however, there are more of other people's interests dependent upon him than almost any other class of subordinates. If he is an amanuensis, and by tardiness, delays his employer's correspondence, even a single mail, it is possible he may, by such neglect, cause the loss of more than he can earn in months or even years.

If he is employed in the courts, or is to make a report of some speech or convention, he may, by not being on time, cause these to be adjourned for the day, involving the loss, it may be, of hundreds of dollars, and, what is far worse, lose his reputation as a prompt and reliable reporter, which, when once lost, will be hard to win back again.

The reporter should always be at his post promptly, and he will find that it will pay him well.

LXXXVII. Always Be Prepared for Work.

Only those who have gone into the court room, or to a lecture, convention, or public meeting, and found, when about to begin work, that they had brought a note-book already filled, or made some similar mistake, will appreciate the value of this suggestion. These little things are very annoying, and are likely to bring a reporter into disfavor, if they occur too frequently. No reporter should ever set out to do any kind of reporting whatever without first examining his note-book and supply of pens and pencils. If a steel pen is used, a few extra pens should be kept about one's person. It is also advisable to keep a few pencils ready sharpened so that should anything occur to necessitate their use the reporter will not be at a loss. It is advisable also that some sort of a pocket inkstand be carried by the reporter, as the ink usually found in a court room, or where public meetings are held, is generally of the vilest sort and by no means fit to use.

The careful reporter will form the habit of always looking after these small yet essential things, and will thus not be obliged to lose the report of some important proceedings.

LXXXVIII. Use a Note-Book Specially Prepared for Shorthand Work.

The size most convenient for practical work is one about five by eight inches, opening at the end with a marginal ruling about an inch from the left side. In ordinary work this space should be left blank so as to give room for insertions and alterations which may be made at any other time. This will be found quite convenient for the amanuensis reporter, who will often be called upon to insert some clause in the body of a letter after it has been dictated, or to change the wording upon some important point. Some reporters make allowances for such changes by writing only upon every other line. This, of course, will serve the purpose, but it is an unnecessary waste of paper, which, in a short time, will amount to considerable.

Note-books bound so that they will lie flat on the desk when open will enable the writer to use both sides of a leaf as he goes along, otherwise it would be necessary to use only one side at first, and then turn and fill the other half. This latter is not a convenient form for reference, and should be avoided.

Some prefer note-books which open at the side. Those opening at the end, however, are more convenient, since it is not possible to have a book opening at the side that will lie perfectly level when open, and, as a result, it is difficult to write near the end of lines on the left page, or the beginning of those on the right.

A note-book with a stiff cover will be found the most convenient. It keeps the paper from being folded or soiled, and when occasion requires you to make a report with no better place than your knee upon which to place your note-book, you will still have a level surface upon which to write.

LXXXIX. Make It a Point to Secure, as Nearly as Possible, the Exact Words of the Speaker.

Beginners are very apt, by trying to get every word before it is possible for them to do so, to fall into the habit of getting a portion only of each sentence. A few entire sentences missed from a speech will not prove nearly as fatal to a good report as to have the latter part of a large number of sentences wanting.

Even if only a brief report is desired, it is much better to take full notes, as it will be easier to prepare it from such than from meagre notes, as more time is given when transcribing to decide upon the relative importance of the different parts of the report. No effort should be made, while taking notes, to correct mere verbal errors which any speaker is liable to make. Though it is the reporter's place to correct all evident mistakes thus made, it can be done better while making the transcript.

As a rule, take down everything just as nearly as possible as it is said, and then, whether a full or only a condensed report is wanted, plenty of material will be at hand from which to draw.

XC. Accustom Yourself to Inconveniences in Reporting.

If you expect to engage in general reporting rather than to confine yourself to any particular line of the work, you will find it quite necessary to accustom yourself to put up with all sorts of inconveniences. Especially in general newspaper work, you will often times be called upon to write in unusual places where there is everything possible to contend with. It may be that you will have to write with your note-book upon your knee, or make use of some other person's back. You may find it necessary to use poor ink on poor paper, or a hard lead pencil on finely calendered paper. It may so happen that you will be obliged to write in almost total darkness. In order to succeed you must be prepared to meet all such emergencies. No matter how careful you may be or how hard you may endeavor to avoid such things, they will occasionally occur, and the only way is to keep your wits about you and make the best of them. Those who are able to do so are the ones who are sure to succeed.

XCI. Any part of a Report Which is Indistinctly Heard Should Be Marked by Some Sign to Indicate the Uncertainty.

A vertical line drawn beside that which is not distinctly heard will be sufficient to call the attention to that part afterwards. Where any portion is entirely lost, a space should be left for it, and a similar sign used to indicate that there is something to be supplied.

When anything of this kind occurs, the reporter should, before making a transcript of the report, endeavor to obtain what was omitted or to ascertain the exact reading of any doubtful passages. If other reporters have made a report of the same proceedings, help may be obtained from them. If not, the speaker, a part of whose speech was lost, may be consulted. If neither of these courses is open, it may be posible to obtain the desired information from some one who was in attendance and who is known to be an attentive listener. It is always better, of course, to be able to make such a report that help of this kind will not be needed.

XCII. In Transcribing Always Read a Full Sentence Before Beginning to Write.

In translating, much help is derived from the context. This being the case, it is quite necessary that a full sentence be read, and often times even more than this, in order to be sure of the meaning.

Beginners who have not acquired a capacity to retain more than a few words in the mind at once are very apt to fall into the habit of translating and then transcribing only very short sentences or parts of long sentences at a time. In this way they are liable to make many mistakes, and to give translations entirely different from what was intended.

A few experiences of this kind will be sufficient to impress upon the young reporter's mind the necessity of looking ahead. He may, however, avoid all difficulty in this direction by heeding this suggestion and profiting by the experience of those who have made similar mistakes.

XCIII. If, When Transcribing, Some Portions of Your Notes Puzzle You, Leave Spaces and Go on, and When You Get the full Sense it Will Be Much Easier to Decipher Them.

The best reporters, like many longhand writers, will sometimes get puzzled over some inaccurately formed character or outline or some sign which may be translated in different ways, each way making complete sense. When a case of this kind occurs, it will be better to leave the difficult part for the time being, since, after reading the balance of the letter or paper and having its complete sense, the chances are that the difficult passage can be easily read. It will be found that the most difficulty is caused by outlines that may be translated in more than one way. Such ambiguities may be avoided by always vocalizing outlines likely to conflict with others. Although it is hard for the beginner, when struggling to keep up with a speaker, to always think just what outlines, if not vocalized, are liable to cause difficulty, yet a little attention tc this point will soon enable him to see instantly just where there is danger of ambiguity, so that some distinguishing vowel may be inserted and all cause for doubt removed.

XCIV. In Making Transcripts, Write Only on One Side of the Paper.

Especially in preparing legal documents, and in writing up reports for publication, only one side of the paper should be used. Business men also generally prefer that only one side of the paper be written upon.

If a letter contains more than can be written on a single sheet, it is best, in order to avoid confusion, to place at the head of the second and following pages the name of the person to whom the letter is written, and after this the number of the page. Thus, in transcribing a letter to Mr. Evans, the second page should be headed

Evans, 2,

and the letter continue immediately below it.

Sometimes it may occur that the person for whom the work is done may wish certain letters to be written on both sides of the paper. Such cases are generally specified. Unless they are, one side only should be used.

XCV. Make All Your Memoranda in Shorthand.

As soon as you are able to apply all the principles correctly, you can not do better than to make all your memoranda in Shorthand. This will help you in several ways. It will develop confidence in your work, a thing which most beginners are very apt to lack. By making note of items upon which something of importance depends, and trusting wholly to your notes for them, you will soon find yourself feeling just as certain of their meaning as you would, were they written in longhand, a feeling which you must have, if you would make a successful reporter. You will also have your private memoranda and accounts in such a form that, should they be lost or mislaid and happen to fall into the hands of others, no advantage ordinarily could be taken of them. Another advantage to be derived from such a habit is in the constant practice which it gives. All are aware of the impression which most people have that unless one is continually practicing the art it will soon be forgotten. This is true only in part, and even this slight objection may be removed by using Shorthand for all private memoranda and note taking. By using it in this way the young Stenographer will soon find that not a day will pass during which he will not have some occasion to make use of it, and by so doing will not allow himself to get rusty in the work.

The greatest advantage, however, of forming the habit of using Shorthand in making memoranda is that, since it can be done so easily and rapidly, one is far more apt to note down many little things which, were it necessary to write them out in longhand, would be neglected altogether. Since it pays, and pays well, to look after the little things, that which will make it possible to do so without too much inconvenience is certainly worthy of some special attention.

XCVI. Numbers Are Generally Represented by the Ordinary Figures or Numerals.

As a rule it will be found best to write all numbers with the ordinary figures, though sometimes it will be shorter to express a number with Shorthand characters. It will generally be found easier to write round numbers, as hundreds, thousands, or millions, in this way. Where a number contains different units, as for instance, tens, hundreds and thousands, it will be easier, and the notes plainer, to write the ordinary Roman numerals. Some reporters never write a figure at all in their Shorthand notes, while others use them exclusively. The majority of reporters, however, use both forms.

XCVII. Preserve Carefully All Shorthand Notes.

If you are a Court reporter, your notes should be indexed, and filed away by the clerk of the court in which the reports are made. If a transcript is made, it is not so essential that the original report be preserved. If not transcribed, they should, in all cases, be carefully filed away, since it is never possible to tell what contingencies may arise. A transcript may never be called for; again, something may take place, years after a report has been made, which will cause it to be of great value. To meet all such contingencies it is quite essential that all reports of legal proceedings should be preserved.

The Amanuensis reporter should adopt some convenient form of note-book, and, for the sake of uniformity, adhere to it. These should be carefully indexed. This index should show name, date, and page on which each letter is written. When a book is filled, the date of the first and last letter contained within it should be marked on the back. Some keep a general index book, showing, first, the names in alphabetical order of all parties to whom letters have been taken at dictation. Opposite the name is placed, first, the number of the note-book, and under each of these are given the different pages on which letters have been written to that particular person. It is not difficult to so index note-books, and much time may be saved thereby. As the reporter is generally expected to look after such things himself, he ought to adopt some definite and practical plan, and then not neglect it, as is too often done.

With all note-books carefully indexed and filed away, one may in a moment's time, refer to all the letters written to any party. As business men often have to refer to letters written at some previous time, they will fully appreciate an arrangement by which they may readily refer to any particular one they may wish to see.

In Speech and Convention reporting, it is not so important that the notes be preserved; yet even with these it often occurs that an old report will be called for, and may prove to be worth far more than the little time required to keep on file all the reports you have ever made.

XCVIII. Take Some Shorthand Magazine.

In this way you will be able to see the work of the best writers, and to get a fair idea of what actual reporting looks like. You will also have an opportunity to practice upon the work of others. This is a valuable exercise for the student, since it not only enables him to read Short-hand writing more readily, but, being matter that is correctly written, it enables him to correct many mistakes which he is in the habit of making, and also recalls many points which would otherwise be forgotten. Almost every one of these magazines contains, besides the Shorthand matter, much valuable information for the student in the line of editorials, contributed articles, and general Shorthand news. They are, as a rule, ably edited and well worth the small price asked for them. In keeping alive an interest in this really beautiful study, a good Shorthand journal is almost, if not quite, equal to a teacher. It is sure to create a deeper interest in the study, since it brings all its readers into closer sympathy, and enables them to reap the benefits of each other's experience. From close observation I have found that those who have become readers of a Shorthand journal are much less apt to become discouraged and give up the study. It is a constant source of encouragement and inspiration to better and more thorough work, which, in the end, is sure to bring success. No Shorthand student should hesitate for a moment about availing himself of the advantages which will certainly be derived from help of this kind.

XCIX. Become a Member of Some Circulating Library or Book Exchange Club.

The average reporter never dreams of how much there really is in the literature of Shorthand, and of the many interesting things there are connected with its history. If you would fully appreciate the progress that has been made, and which is daily being carried further, you should give some attention to the literature of the art. To have a proper appreciation of the profession of which you are a member, you must understand its history, and know something of its struggles and its triumphs. Until you do this, your views will be narrow and your efforts restricted.

As it is a slow and expensive task to accumulate a large and well selected library on any subject, very few are able to do so. Shorthand writers need not, however, be deprived of the privilege of enjoying all that has been written concerning the art. By taking advantage of the opportunities offered by some circulating library which has been established for the benefit of Shorthand writers, one may for a very small sum, have access to almost any work that has ever been published on the subject of brief writing.

The American Exchange Club is, no doubt, the best of the kind. The catalogue contains a very large list of rare and valuable books and magazines, any of which may be had by members of the club.

C. Avoid the Evil Effects of Such Stimulants as Tobacco and Strong Drink.

Success in Shorthand writing, like success in any other of the finer manual arts, depends primarily upon the healthy action of the nervous system. It is important, then, that the reporter, requiring, as he does, clearness of thought with rapidity of execution, should carefully avoid anything that tends to throw the nervous system out of its natural condition. Since the chief effect of alcohol is upon the nerves, caused by its being an irritant and retarding digestion, by affecting the cardinal nerves and increasing the rapidity of the circulation, and by being a cerebral poison, thus affecting the reason, it should be scrupulously avoided by the reporter. Though it may result sometimes in arousing one to greater activity and greater efforts for the time being, yet this temporary exaltation of the brain under its influence is inevitably succeeded by a state of relaxation which soon ends in nervous and physical debility.

The effect of tobacco, though not so great, is in the same direction. It is an unhealthy stimulant, the evil effects greatly overbalancing the little apparent good that may be derived from its use. The reporter who rigidly abstains from the use of both tobacco and alcohol may be assured that his chances of success are much greater than the one addicted to them.

Note.—The following table gives the number of words in each suggestion in the book. This is given for the purpose of speed work in practice.

I	227	XXVI	368	LI	203	LXXVI	192
II	296	XXVII	278	LII	275	LXXVII	179
III	221	XXVIII	185	LIII	207	LXXVIII	291
IV	386	XXIX	99	LIV	223	LXXIX	212
V	160	XXX	317	LV	273	LXXX	143
VI	196	XXXI	218	LVI	229	LXXXI	200
VII	169	XXXII	440	LVII	302	LXXXII	261
VIII	309	XXXIII	266	LVIII	103	LXXXIII	198
IX	443	XXXIV	257	LIX	97	LXXXIV	283
X	375	XXXV	136	LX	319	LXXXV	224
XI	118	XXXVI	258	LXI	403	LXXXVI	214
XII	229	XXXVII	408	LXII	215	LXXXVII	210
XIII	302	XXXVIII	145	LXIII	173	LXXXVIII	315
XIV	164	XXXIX	224	LXIV	211	LXXXIX	193
XV	408	XL	324	LXV	166	XC	188
XVI	372	XLI	207	LXVI	264	XCI	167
XVII	240	XLII	194	LXVII	161	XCII	148
XVIII	252	XLIII	333	LXVIII	146	XCIII	179
XIX	230	XLIV	262	LXIX	109	XCIV	149
XX	388	XLV	221	LXX	218	XCV	331
XXI	246	XLVI	410	LXXI	206	XCVI	99
XXII	296	XLVII	328	LXXII	189	XCVII	389
XXIII	177	XLVIII	171	LXXIII	239	XCVIII	266
XXIV	107	XLIX	239	LXXIV	343	XCIX	226
XXV	239	L	183	LXXV	146	C	215

HOME STUDY.

"PUT YOUR GOLD INTO YOUR HEAD AND NO ONE CAN TAKE IT FROM YOU."

CENTRAL COLLEGE OF CORRESPONDENCE,
ST. LOUIS, MO.

New Copyrighted Method of Teaching by Mail. Eleven Hundred Students enrolled; 140 in Ohio; 90 in Pennsylvania; 70 in Indiana; 50 in Illinois; 40 in New York; 40 in Missouri, etc.

BRANCHES TAUGHT:

BOOK-KEEPING,   COMMERCIAL LAW,
   TELEGRAPHY,   DRAWING,
      SHORTHAND,   ALGEBRA,
         PENMANSHIP,   GEOMETRY,
PRACTICAL   PHYSIOLOGY,
   ARITHMETIC,   HISTORY;
      COMMERCIAL   LANGUAGE,
         ARITHMETIC,   POLITICAL
            ORTHOGRAPAY,   ECONOMY,
               GRAMMAR,   ETC.
COMPOSITION AND LETTER WRITING.

TERMS for Complete Course, $5 to $20 per single branch. Liberal discount when more than two branches are pursued. Diplomas awarded. Shorthand Trial Lessons Free. Moran Method. Pitman System.

TEACHING BY MAIL

Has been demonstrated to be thoroughly practical, and is a grand success. It is cheap, convenient and economical—*the Method of the fnture*. Write for particulars. No charge.
   Address,

COLLEGE OF CORRESPONDENCE,
SEVENTEENTH AND OLIVE STS.,   ST. LOUIS, MO.

CARBON PAPER

For making two to twenty copies at one writing, with or without writing machines.

Beckwith Carbon Paper,

Best and cheapest, $2.10 per 100 sheets, legal size, postage paid, or 30 cents per dozen, postage paid.

Linen Paper legal size for making six copies at one writing, $1.30 per ream.

Typewriter Supplies. Send for Circular.

T. J. BECKWITH,

701 East State St.,   MARSHALL, MICH.

ESTABLISHED 1862.

*T*HE experience of the past three years has proved our "Perfection" FOUNTAIN PEN to be the best and most reliable. It is made of the best rubber and has a full size John Holland 16 kr Gold Pen, put up in a handsome Morocco Box with filler, making the largest and best Fountain Pen sold for $2.50 each. For sale by the Trade and the Manufacturers, The John Holland Gold Pen Company, 19 WEST FOURTH ST., CINCINNATI, Manufacturers of all styles of best quality Gold Pens, Pencils, Pen-Holders and Fountain Pens. Special attention to repairs.

Serrated Edge Ribbons

For all kinds of Type-Writers, guaranteed satisfactory or money refunded. This improved edge prevents much of the curling complained of in other kinds of ribbons, gives an equal appearance the whole width of the ribbon, and will not fray or ravel.

*   *   *   *   *

Carbon Papers

For Type-Writers and Stylus, that will not dry out under any circumstances, however much exposed to the air. In all colors and sizes. Every sheet guaranteed to be as represented, or may be returned and money refunded.

For Catalogue or sample, address,

A. P. LITTLE, MFR.,

Rochester, N. Y.

ROCKWELL & RUPEL
OF CHICAGO.

☞ AGREE:—For the purpose of securing a trial order from every stenographer engaged in active service, in the United States and elsewhere, on application we will forward to any stenographer in the world, 1 dozen sheets of Black, Purple, Blue, Green, or Red Carbon Paper 8x12, and one Black, Blue, Purple, Green, or Red Record or Copying Ribbon for any writing machine, for

$1.25 IN CASH, Postage Paid.

Rockwell & Rupel,
OF CHICAGO.

☞ FURTHER AGREE, That in case goods ordered do not give absolute satisfaction; if they do not do everything we claim in our advertisements; or if it is found that ANY CLAIM WE MAKE is not wholly true in every respect, we will refund DOUBLE THE RETAIL PRICE OF THESE GOODS which is as follows:

Remington	Ribbons,	$9.00	per doz.
Caligraph	"	7.00	"
Hammond	"	9.00	"
Smith-Premier	"	9.00	"
Crandall	"	6.00	"
Munson	"	9.00	"
Carbon Paper, any color,		4.00	per 100 sheets.

Rockwell & Rupel,
94-96 LaSalle Street,
CHICAGO.

You are to be your own judge of these goods. Your word will be good and your money will be refunded as per agreement if found unsatisfactory.

As to our RESPONSIBILITY we refer to:

Any Typewriter Agency in Chicago. Any Law Stenographer in Chicago, Racine or Milwaukee.

Union National Bank, Racine, Wis.

Manufacturers' National Bank, Racine, Wis.

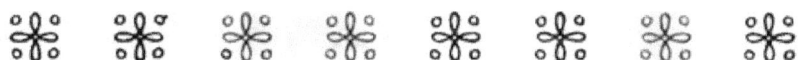

REPORTERS'
NOTE BOOKS

We will send you, postpaid, a first class Reporters' Note Book, containing **220** pages, 6 x 9 inches, of good Calendered Paper with cloth sides and leather back for

ONLY 35 CENTS.

THREE FOR $1.00.

Similar Books usually sell for from sixty to seventy-five cents each. This is the best bargain of the season. Send for a trial order. We are sure our books will please you.

Address,

STENOGRAPHIC INSTITUTE,

Ann Arbor, Mich.

Boyd's Automatic Type Cleaner.

It is *adjusted instantly without touching the ribbon or removing the work from the machine* and the type are thoroughly and quickly cleaned by a few strokes of each key in the usual manner.

This is really an ingenious contrivance, and yet nothing could be simpler. The curved steel brush handle snaps on to the front part of the machine, bringing the brush right over the center of the basket and under the ribbon. The keys are then each struck a few times, rapidly; this brings the face of the type against the stiff bristles of the brush which revolves by the motion of the keys and thoroughly cleans the type. Every type can with this brush be cleaned in less than two minutes. Send for one. We will mail you one, postpaid, for 25c.

Address

STENOGRAPHIC INSTITUTE,

Ann Arbor, Mich.

STENOGRAPHIC PENCILS !

THE BEST IN THE MARKET.

——— THESE PENCILS WERE ———

Made especially for our use.

And are *Warranted by us*

As being *Unsurpassed for Office Use.*

75 cts. per dozen. Sent by mail postpaid.

Address S. A. MORAN,   Ann Arbor, Mich.

THE REPORTING STYLE

—OF—

SHORTHAND

—BY—

ELDON MORAN,

Formerly Principal Iowa State University SCHOOL OF SHORTHAND.

The new edition, the eleventh, of **this work is the very latest and** best text book extant. It is selling faster than any other work of **the** kind in print. Its great merit is in having the *subject of Shorthand explained so completely* **that** *anyone can understand it.* The **book** also contains lessons on Amanuensis, Speech, and Court Reporting.

This book deals exclusively with that part of Shorthand **actually** necessary for practical purposes. The so-called Corresponding Style and the method of first learning to write words in one way and afterwards in a different manner, as taught in *every other work on Shorthand* are entirely discarded. To learn first a long way of writing a word and afterwards a **more brief** method proves **a serious** obstacle to the reporter, since a person in attempting to do a thing quickly, as is necessary in reporting, is very apt to make use of the first outline learned even though it may require a much longer time. To overcome this habit a person must unlearn the first method, a thing which is in a measure impossible.

This book makes a vast saving to the student, usually enabling him to master the art and begin work in one-half the time which the ordinary text-books require. This book has met with such flattering success that the eleventh edition is now (May, 1890) nearly exhausted. No other shorthand book is in such great demand. Send for a copy, for you will never regret it. Book sent, postpaid, for $1.50.

Address

S. A. MORAN,

Ann Arbor, Mich.

3000
COMMERCIAL PHRASES

ADAPTED TO THE

PITMAN AND GRAHAM SYSTEMS

OF SHORTHAND.

—BY—

GEO. W. HALL,

STENOGRAPHER Chicago, Milwaukee & St. Paul R. R.

THIRD EDITION.—COPYRIGHTED.

Every Stenographer should have this book. The Phrases are nicely engraved, easily read, and of easy reference, being alphabetically arranged, and with the long hand opposite each phrase. **You** will never regret the small sum necessary to get the book. *Send for it at once.* **Orders** *promptly filled.* Price, postpaid, 75 cents.

Address STENOGRAPHIC INSTITUTE,

Ann Arbor, Mich.

AN AID

IN THE ACQUISITION OF

GRAHAM'S SHORTHAND

BY ALFRED DAY.

Are you studying Graham's "Hand Book"? Then you should have this book by all means. It will save you an immense amount of time, labor and energy. It is clear and concise and makes an excellent "short-cut" to the end of Mr. Graham's complicated work, at the same time introducing *everything that is essential.* Every teacher of the Graham system should have a copy. Price, postage prepaid, 75c.

Address THE STENOGRAPHIC INSTITUTE,

Ann Arbor, Mich.

PRACTICAL TYPEWRITING

By BATES TORREY.

This work teaches **The All Finger Method.** This is the

PIONEER TEXT-BOOK in the NEW ERA

— OF —

WRITING BY TOUCH.

IT CONTAINS ABOUT

A Thousand Suggestions about Typewriting

— AND —

ORNAMENTAL WORK.

It is indeed **AN EPITOME** of **TYPEWRITER POSSIBILITY** and is **INDISPENSABLE TO BEGINNERS, OPERATORS, EVERYBODY.**

SUMMARY OF CONTENTS.

Utility of the Writing Machine (opinions of notable people).—Typewriters and Typewriting.—Improvement in Procedure.—A Practical Method.—Advantages of the All-Finger Method.—Writing by Touch Foreshadowed.—Advice of an Expert.

Position at Machine.—The Touch.—Finger Action.—General Remarks.—Lesson I.—First Tasks.—Preliminary Practice.—Exceptional Fingering.—Further Remarks.

Diagram of Key Board.—Finger Exercises.—Right and Left Hand Practice.—Graded Words.—Common Words.—Pertinent Advice.—Prefixes and Affixes.

Curious Combinations.—Illustrative Words.—The Numerals.—Tabular Work with Full Explanation.—Miscellaneous Words Figured.—Commercial, Legal, and Anatomical Terms.—McGurrin's List.

Simple Sentence Practice.—Proximity.—Chain Sentences.—Touch Practice.—Testimony and Rhyme.—Forms for Letter, Billhead, etc.

General Instruction. Care of Machine.—Advice about Everything Allied to Typewriters and Their Work.—Particular Instruction.—The Minutiæ of Typewriter Management.—Expedients and How Managed.—Numerous Devices.—Additional Matter of Importance.

Typewriting by Mail.—Common-sense Punctuation.—Use of the Stops as Applied to Writing Machine.—Eccentricities of Typewriter Punctuation.—A Scheme of Abbreviated Longhand (standard).

A Chapter of Ornamental Typewriting.—Fancy Borders, Tail Pieces, and the Like.—Titles, Captions, Legal Forms, and Otherwise.—A Variety of Writing Machine Possibilities.

If you expect to make a success of typewriting, do not fail to secure a copy of this book. It is highly recommended by every professional typewriter operator in the country.

Price, Elegantly Bound in Cloth, Postpaid, $1.50.

Address S. A. MORAN,   Ann Arbor, Michigan.

www.ingramcontent.com/pod-product-compliance
Lightning Source LLC
Chambersburg PA
CBHW030620270326
41927CB00007B/1252